CAUGHT IN FADING LIGHT

GARY THORP

WALKER & COMPANY

New York

CAUGHT IN FADING LIGHT

Mountain Lions, Zen Masters,

and Wild Nature

First published in the United States of America in 2002 by Walker Publishing Company, Inc.

For information about permission to reproduce selections from this book, write to Permissions, Walker & Company, 435 Hudson Street, New York, New York 10014

Library of Congress Cataloging-in-Publication Data available upon request
ISBN 0-8027-1397-1 (hardcover)

The quote on page 8 is from "Breakthroughs in Weird Science" *San Francisco Chronicle*, July 31, 2000. Copyright 2000 by the *San Francisco Chronicle*. Used with permission of the *San Francisco Chronicle* and Copyright Clearance Center. Gary Snyder quotation on page 35 is from "A Place in Space: Ethics, Aesthetics, and Watersheds" *Counterpoint*, Washington, D.C. Copyright 1995 Gary Snyder. Used with permission. Excerpt from the unpublished journals of Chiura Obata on pages 74–75, used with the permission of Kimi Kodami Hill and the Estate of Chiura Obata. Excerpt from "Environmental Practice at Green Gulch Zen Center" on pages 100–01, reprinted with the permission of San Francisco Zen Center. The poem "Traveling Through the Dark" copyright 1962, 1998 by the Estate of William Stafford on pages 116–17 is reprinted from *The Way It Is: New & Selected Poems* with the permission of Graywolf Press, Saint Paul, Minnesota.

Visit Walker & Company's Web site at www.walkerbooks.com

Book design by Katy Riegel

Illustrations by Martie Holmer

Printed in the United States of America

2   4   6   8   10   9   7   5   3   1

Following a path takes more than footsteps.
—Hsieh Ling-yun

The greatest enemy of any pursuit is reason.
—Jose Ortega y Gasset

Contents

Part Two:

MOUNTAINS ARE NOT
WHAT THEY SEEM

Part Three:
MOUNTAINS ARE MOUNTAINS
ONCE AGAIN

PREFACE

ONE EVENING, not long after the six o'clock
news had ended, I decided that I would go out and
find a mountain lion. The news broadcast that night
was not enough on its own to send me out the door,
but it seemed to mark a turning point, an indication
that changes in my life were imminent. Watching this
undistinguished newscast had pointed me toward
restlessness and to a growing sense that something in
my life was beginning to slip away. The format of the
news program had grown so formulaic over the years
that I felt blunted and dulled by what I watched. I
sensed that I might be losing my capacity to ever be
surprised again. The manner in which television news
was delivered was predictable and manipulative; the
string of serious beginnings, the teasers before commercial breaks, the smiles and chuckles that followed
the final, heartwarming story. As I watched that
night, I wondered whether parts of my own life hadn't
also grown routine. There were people, I knew, who
had seen the magician's trick performed one too many
times and who were thereafter skeptical of much of
what they saw. Whether I'd seen too much or too little
wasn't clear to me, but I felt that, at least for a time, I
needed to observe things in a radically different way.

The world news was only part of it. As the faces of
the newsmakers were revealed on the screen that
night, I thought of friends who had come and gone

in my own life, of jobs not taken, books not read, of decisions made in haste that had produced unseen results. Although my life was relatively pleasant, I began to consider the things I'd missed, the elusive times that might have been, the simple actions that could have altered an entire course of events, the countless moments that had gone by unnoticed.

Years earlier, a similar yearning to more deeply experience life's events had led me to the study of Zen Buddhism. Many of Zen's lessons had stayed with me. I had found these teachings invaluable in honing my rather uneven powers of observation and concentration throughout the years. Over and over, the teachers had emphasized the importance of looking at things clearly and objectively. Yet, it was said, these skills could never be attained in any rashly impetuous or offhand fashion. Only through constant practice, with patience and deliberateness, could one be drawn to the desired objective.

But what was my objective? I seemed not to have any. I had lived the life of a student, a musician, and a businessman, and had experienced the breakup of one marriage and the enjoyment of another that was long-lasting and successful. These events in my life were important milestones, but it seemed to me that the true richness of one's life was often created in the lesser moments now forgotten.

Earlier in the day, a friend had seen a mountain lion in the hills above our town. This was merely one of many such reports I'd heard described through the years. I had never seen one of these animals myself, and it occurred to me then that I might go out and find one. Often I had considered doing this in the past, but the pressures of time and work had always intervened. I wasn't exactly certain why this appeared so important to me now. I was wary of the sudden impulse, yet at the same time I could feel myself growing enlivened at the very prospect of looking for one of these lions. I didn't see this search as either a makeshift expedient or an irrevocable undertaking, and I was quite certain that some of the reasons for what I was about to take on would become clearer as I went along. At the very least, I could become more familiar with the territory in which I lived. I could begin to walk my own home ground. Being actively engaged in this kind of enterprise seemed to be exactly what was called for.

I was not at all knowledgeable as to how much time would be required to conduct a pursuit such as this, nor did I know how much time I was prepared to give it. In fact, there were a great many things I didn't know regarding what I was about to do. At the time, I supposed that *any* new undertaking might have some dubious factors that could be detrimental to one's aim, but these few misgivings and uncertainties seemed only to add to the attractiveness of my own venture.

Poets have said that crows and ravens need no shadows; they already *are* shadows. To write about mountain lions is, at best, to produce a series of shadows. There is no hope of ever, on paper, revealing the true animal. There's a long list of gifted writers who have written well about mountain lions: Barry Lopez, Edward Hoagland, Ed Abbey, Rick Bass, Terry Tempest Williams, Jack Turner, and others; but they have written about *their* mountain lions. There is a tradition at work here; a record of various individuals trying to describe a creature only briefly seen; the written depiction of shadows that, when there is sufficient light and conditions are right, might chance to cross our own.

In Japanese literature, the form of writing known as *nikki bungaku* has a centuries-long tradition. These literary diaries or journals are composed of separate, yet interrelated, short narratives that proceed in a continuous line from beginning to end, and which tell a sort of story. They contain nothing extra and are complete as they are. Historically, the *nikki* form has always been quite liberating for writers. In its pages, a writer can behave as he or she wishes. The writing can consist wholly, or contain elements, of poetry, fiction, or nonfiction. Indeed, there have been male diarists who wrote as women, charlatans who wrote as Zen masters, and poets who wrote as uneducated vagabonds. A writer's craft and imagination are the only limiting factors, regardless of whether one is recording the mundane facts of an average day or journeying across a land never visited before. When poetry is produced, it is offered, not as embellishment, but as one of the natural facts of daily life.

When I set out to find a mountain lion, and to write about my experience, I anticipated that many other topics would be encountered along the way. Years of hiking and mountain climbing, and my time as a Zen student, would certainly influence whatever I had to say. A simple notebook or daily journal seemed inadequate to the task. In writing about my search for cougars, I found inspiration in the *nikki* style, but attempted to rid the resultant narrative of any artificial fabrication. This kind of writing might also be called *zuihitsu,* or "chasing the writing brush." The simplicity of this style and its seeming lack of structure allow the writer (and the reader) to move forward in a single, controlled line.

The book I have written about my search for cougars is divided into three sections, not because of any break in what actually occurred, but because there were three distinct and different ways in which I caught myself looking.

What follows, then, is a record of my experience as I went out trying to find a mountain lion. Although the search described may be an elusive one, the writing is as unshadowed and as true as I can make it.

PART ONE

MOUNTAINS ARE
JUST MOUNTAINS

SEGAKI AND DRIVING HOME

This was no dream.

THERE WERE LIONS and dragons. There was a fish, a pig, an ancient and skeletal bearded sage, and two Buddhas. They were all beating drums, blowing horns and conch shells, striking wooden clackers, and pounding on overturned buckets and plastic dishpans. This was the ceremony known as Segaki. It was held in this Zen Buddhist temple once each year, and it was happening this year on Halloween.

People were gathered in the meditation hall to welcome the restless spirits of animals, Buddha ancestors, departed friends and family members, and other beings they could not see. Tables were laden with fruits, vegetables, and flowers to draw these spirits near. Sweet incense was offered; and after the chanting of the Kan Ro Mon and the Dai Hi Shin Dharani, the names of the recently deceased relatives and friends of those present were read. Reading these names aloud, publicly, was an expression both of acknowledgment and of respect. And as this assembly was of a fair size, the list of names was long.

We were at the Green Dragon Temple, a part of Green Gulch Farm Zen Center, just thirty minutes north of San Francisco. I had spent the afternoon in the hills above, looking for signs of a mountain lion. Green Gulch is one place, among very few, where it is possible to encounter both Zen teaching and wild cougars in the same afternoon. Throughout the years, there have been occasional cougar sightings on the surrounding hillsides and on the trails and dirt roads nearby. Once, one of these cats was seen resting near the edge of the large pond just outside the meditation hall. There was nothing unusual about the presence of a wild animal in this area, as it is the natural habitat of deer, raccoons, and gray foxes, as well as many smaller mammals. It seemed only natural that a person might spot a visiting cougar here from time to time.

Rick Fields, who wrote *How the Swans Came to the Lake*, a history of Buddhism in America, was one of those who saw a mountain lion here. Rick was out for a daytime walk when the animal appeared before him. Shortly after they'd seen each other, the cougar had dropped down into a patch of coyote bush just below the edge of the hillside trail. Rick went to investigate. Slowly and carefully, he made his approach, waiting to see when the cougar might erupt from the brush and break into the open. As he neared the bush, he could see that the animal was no longer there. It had disappeared right before his eyes.

During the past year, Rick had died of cancer; and it happened that his name was one of those read in the *zendo* that afternoon. As I drove home from the ceremony that Halloween evening, I thought of the people I'd known whose names had been read. I thought about cancer, and I thought about cougars. The chances of being killed by a mountain lion were much less great than being struck by lightning. Yet people had died in this manner. As I drove down the mountain, I tried to recall and recite some of their names; Lucy Gomez, Scott Lancaster, Barbara Schoener, Iris Kenna, Steven Parolin, Mark Miedema. I had known none of these unfortunates, but I continued to recite their names from memory.

The air grew cooler, and the sky darker, as I wished the departed spirits of these people rest.

2

THE CAGE

A WEEK OR so later, I was standing as close to a mountain lion as I had ever been. She took a half dozen steps and then turned quickly in the opposite direction. She walked directly toward a seemingly invisible point, then whirled around and came back toward me. After stopping, she took another six steps and began the same routine all over again. Time after time, she repeated her unvarying circuit. She never looked up from the hard-packed floor of her enclosure. She didn't know that I was standing five feet away from her. She didn't care.

This kind of ritualistic pacing is known as stereotypy. The repetitive motions are mechanical, and they have no apparent function or goal. Relentless walking while oblivious to one's surroundings is a sign of unrest, even turmoil, common to human beings as well as captive animals, and I was trying hard not to identify too much with the animal before me. Her pacing reminded me of much of the routine nature of my own life; the constricting priorities; the countless looping departures and returns; the constant, repetitive motions that seemed to have questionable benefit. Still, it was important that I pay this visit, that I get as close as possible to an example of what I was going looking for.

I had never been a frequent visitor of zoos or wild animal parks, but had come specifically to see this large cat. She was nearly twenty years of age, about as long as mountain lions (also known as cougars or pumas) usually live. Were she still in the wild, she would be lucky to have reached half this age.

I had come to pay my respects as well as to get a close look at her. This cougar had once stalked me, from the other side of the chain-link barrier. She had just been moved here, and compared to where she had been kept before, this compound seemed new and sizable to her. Unfamiliar with the reality of her limitations, she had seemed unaware that she was behind a fence at all and crouched low to the ground, never taking her eyes from me. As slowly as a shadow, she moved toward me, the tip of her tail twitching violently, her teeth clattering like castanets, her power fully restrained. This might have all been done in the spirit of play. I'll simply never know. But I do know that, even with the presence of interposed steel wire fencing, I felt something in the back of my neck that I'll never be able to describe.

On that occasion, except for her clicking teeth, the cougar had been absolutely silent. But I'd heard of people who had, after being followed by mountain lions in the wild, later commented that the animals had made "coughing" sounds. This raised questions, once again, concerning the animal's real purpose. We are made curious as to whether the cougars might be coughing from nervousness or embarrassment, or whether they're announcing themselves and offering an early warning of their presence. A cougar is certainly capable of maintaining absolute and long-lasting silence; and it seems clear that, should they wish to truly attack, they could (and would) do so without ever making a sound.

I HAD NEVER seen a mountain lion in the wild, but I had come close. One early morning, when my wife and I were camped at Crane Flat Campground in Yosemite, a park ranger told us that he had just seen a pair of mountain lions walking casually past our tent. They had crossed our campsite, six feet from where we were sleeping. The ranger showed us the two sets of tracks clearly imprinted in the dust and early-morning dew, the first tracks of this sort that either my wife or I had ever seen.

At home a few weeks later, a close neighbor reported seeing a young mountain lion crossing the road near our house. Other friends told us of seeing these animals when they went out for early-morning or late-evening walks.

But in years of hiking and hill climbing in the most remote sections of backcountry near us, at all times of night and day, in all possible weather conditions, and whether walking or sitting quietly, we had never seen any sign that these animals existed. It began to rankle. I knew that they were there.

Everybody knew that they were there. But like most things, some people saw them, and some people didn't.

SCIENTISTS TELL us that the universe is expanding at a steadily accelerating rate. However, I am not that kind of scientist. I am interested in mountain lions, not in the vaulted structures of modern physics. Still, I felt my reason imperiled when, in a morning newspaper, I read the following editorial:

> Theoretical physics has taken a couple of big steps into weird territory with recent discoveries that are likely to change the way we look at the universe.
>
> The journal *Nature* reports that scientists at the NEC Research Institute in Princeton, N.J., sent a laser pulse through a vacuum chamber faster than the speed of light.
>
> So fast was the pulse that it exited the chamber even before entering, raising mind-bending questions about cause and effect.
>
> The experiment also challenged Albert Einstein's theory of relativity and the fundamental tenet of physics that nothing travels faster than light, 186,282 miles per second.
>
> Then, a team of scientists at the Fermi National Accelerator Laboratory near Chicago announced that they have found the first direct evidence of the tau neutrino, a ghostly subatomic particle believed to be the final puzzle piece in the make-up of all matter everywhere in the cosmos.

Tau neutrinos are so tiny that trillions of them are blown off the sun every second and pass through Earth—and humans—daily without harm and barely leaving a trace.

Neither superluminal light propagation nor the tau neutrino find has any immediate practical application, scientists say. But they are very good things to know about anyway.

Reading this concise Monday-morning report left me disquieted. I had never considered the possibility of something being able to leave a place before it had arrived. Not even a mountain lion. Nor had I envisioned detectable particles (ghostly or not) continually passing through my body or my world.

I had spent years as a Zen student, and had learned the rules of cause and effect, and examined the notion of "emptiness" and the ever-changing nature of the universe. However, I'd never given physics even a cursory glance.

My scientific interests had always been in natural history: mountain lion ecology, helping to restore the local salmon habitat, propagating endangered native plants, and the like. I had always steered far and wide of the hard sciences: chemistry, geology, physics, astronomy, and math. I had nearly flunked college chemistry because I had decided that I could pass the final exams without ever learning the periodic table of the elements. My professor convinced me that this was folly.

Even though I had no interest in dissecting things or in studying their molecular makeup, I pursued courses in natural history and eastern philosophy. Both of these fields allowed and encouraged one's programmed ways of thinking to break apart and then fall, gently, back into place again. They were designed for those interested in exploring the unexpected and unseen.

It seemed to me that worthwhile discoveries were often made when we sought something quite undefined. I began looking for mountain lions near my home after I had seen evidence of their tracks and scat. This kind of evidence engenders theory; the clear reasoning that if an environment contains such-and-such, then so-and-so must be in it. Even sub-atomic particles had been discovered in this way. The records of their travels had been mapped, disturbances around them had been noted, and their physical properties had been predicted long before they were, in actuality, ever seen or proven to exist.

IT SEEMED only natural, as I stood before that circumambulating lion, that I might someday see one of these animals in the wild. I watched her actions for any sort of clue. I regarded the size of her forepaws. I memorized the shape of her head. And as I stood there, she looked up for the briefest of moments, and noticed that I was there. After acknowledging my existence, she began her circled walking once again. I watched her a while longer and then, shaken by her direct stare, I pulled a notebook from my shoulder pack and wrote down the first twenty random words that came to my mind: redolent, rigorous, verdure, effulgent, implausible, feeble, incendiary, situated, concealed, interstice, filigree, interlace, extirpation, ambiguity, inconspicuous, escarpment, timorous, tangled, oblivious, wishful.

I had no idea if these words meant anything, or, for that matter, if they ever would mean anything. But writing them down seemed a way of beginning.

3

MOONLIGHT

MY NOTEBOOK was a recent acquisition. I had begun carrying it with me everywhere. I did not yet consider myself a writer, but I found it useful for jotting down undeveloped thoughts or random words. It seemed a way of isolating a dull and fleeting notion from one that might later be important.

The first long notations in my journal were written by moonlight, while I was scrunched down uncomfortably in the midst of a serpentine outcrop high up on one of California's coastal mountains. The moon was bright enough that night that I could use its light to write by as I sat there waiting. Below me, the landscape resembled a huge, unwrapped parcel of darkness. I sat among the rocks, waiting for a mountain lion to pass by, or for the inevitable light of dawn to eventually uncover all the hills and streams below.

The snow-white pages I wrote upon contrasted sharply with the dark shadows of my hand and pen. The writing came from nowhere, and was then revealed in the moonlight. The words were drawn from nonexistence onto the snowy page. I realized that in this way, with luck, a person might also draw himself from darkness into light, one word at a time.

MOUNTAIN LIONS and darkness have always gone together. Although sometimes seen in daylight, the cats are most often nocturnal or crepuscular, active either in darkness or semidarkness. Their night vision is ten times greater than that of man.

Many scientists revere and study the speed of light, but what is the speed of darkness? What is the speed of the unseen? Darkness is already everywhere at once, and light is but a momentary interruption.

I remembered hearing of a backcountry Park Service ranger who was cleaning up after dinner one evening when he heard a chilling scream. He ran out of his cabin in time to see a mountain lion standing with a dead deer next to her. The lion saw the ranger and bounded off. The ranger realized that this might be a rare opportunity to closely observe a mountain lion, so he stationed himself a short distance away from the deer carcass. He sat in absolute silence, and listened closely as night deepened. After sitting in darkness for well over an hour, he gave up hope of the lion's returning and stood up. In the powerful beam of his flashlight, he could clearly see that the dead deer was no longer there. The mountain lion had returned and then disappeared again while carrying off her one-hundred-pound burden. She never made the slightest sound.

There is a Confucian proverb: The most difficult thing there is, is to find a black cat in a darkened room, especially when there is no cat.

4

SETTING A GOAL

WHEN THE WRITER Peter Matthiessen was traveling in Nepal in the autumn of 1973, searching for the snow leopard, and after he had trekked for months over some of the highest and most difficult terrain on the planet, he began to have mixed feelings about finding one. For some people, he realized, it was a remarkable experience to see a rare animal, such as a great cat, in its wild environment. For others, it was wonderful *not* to see it. Some of us admire the skill of the creature in traveling unseen and in living among human residents undetected. This is what Matthiessen comprehended; that the search itself was often the most instructive and valuable part of the experience; that this kind of endeavor pitted camouflage and stealth against vision and determination; and that it honed the skills and perceptions of both the pursuer and the prey.

It was wonder and curiosity that had sent Matthiessen on his quest, from thousands of miles away, just to seek a glimpse of the Himalayan snow leopard; and it was also a type of spiritual pilgrimage. To follow something skillfully and with diligence is certainly one of life's great arts. To trace a fragrance, a fragile thread of evidence, an indistinct path, or a new kind of reasoning to a definitive end can be the beginning of a true journey. We must exercise care not to be lured in an illogical direction. Whether we are looking for an elusive cat or a more stationary, less evasive subject, we must use our eyes and heart.

To begin any kind of search is to venture into the

abstract. Our goal may seem well defined to us, but goals are often remote and misleading. They can be weakened renderings of what we're really looking for. Things that call for us to find them can only be imagined things, idealized things. If we find them, they may be, or may not be, what we imagined; but the search itself is always an exercise in being alive. We are gripped by a new kind of energy, and lifted by our own intelligence and innate curiosity.

The thinkers of the world have always advised us to be careful in choosing what we seek. There is danger implied in any new exploration. We are warned, especially, to be wary of the goal that changes shape before our very eyes.

SETTING ALL THESE heavy cautions aside, I had decided that night, after watching the news, to see if I might learn more about mountain lions; to gather information from people who had seen or studied them, to follow a cougar's tracks if possible, and to see this animal in its home environment.

I wondered how a person with my meager abilities could best pursue this undertaking. Clearly, if I wanted to gain any real understanding of mountain lions, I was going to need more than just random luck or desultory study. I was not a trained field biologist, nor was I a hunter or tracker. I was not known for possessing any heightened capabilities in the art of getting close to people without their knowledge. I didn't think of myself as being particularly stealthy, devious, or oblique. I was far from expert in the subtleties of sideways approach. How would I ever get near a mountain lion?

As often happens in life, the facts themselves were difficult to face. The mountain lion is designed to avoid detection. Its sensory abilities are vastly superior to my own. Its senses of hearing, smell, and vision are extraordinary. Its life depends on these abilities to capture food and to elude its enemies. It seems an expert at legerdemain.

The fields and mountains where I live are tawny gold—in fact, lion-colored—for much of the year. A mountain lion can easily rest in the grass undetected. During late autumn, winter, or early spring, after the heavy rains have soaked the coastal hills, everything turns a lush and verdant green. This time of year, a mountain lion might be a bit more visible against its background, but any contrast in colors would be completely negated at night, when the cat was most likely to be in the open. After midnight on a moonless night, the animal could be fluorescent yellow and I would still never see it.

It was clear that, to find a mountain lion, I would need a plan of action. My goal was to meet one of these animals in its own world, to acknowledge it, and move on. This seemed a reasonable enough ambition for a person of my character.

5

NAMES

THE MOUNTAIN LION has been said to have more names than any other animal on Earth. Its original range, which covered much of the western hemisphere, sent it traveling through various human languages, from the southern Yukon to deep in South America. There were words in English, Spanish, Portuguese, French-Canadian, Cajun, and countless other indigenous native languages and dialects for this animal. In the United States alone, the terms *lion, mountain lion, cougar, puma, catamount, panther, painter, screamer, hellcat, ghost cat,* and others are still in use. Even when one seeks these animals in the index of a book, one must be prepared to scurry quickly from word to word.

The taxonomy of the scientific community is also at odds when trying to classify this particular carnivore. For decades, textbooks have called the cougar *Felis concolor,* the cat of one color. When this was changed, a few years ago, to *Puma concolor,* huge numbers of researchers, field biologists, and zoologists refused to make the change. This persistence should not come as any great surprise to anyone who has dealt with those who spend the majority of their lives near wild animals.

To risk further confusion, it must also be noted that the mountain lion is not truly a lion, as is the African lion. Nor is it confined to mountains. It does quite well in a wide variety of habitats, including mountains and foothills, unimpeded deserts, rain forests, swamps, and areas near freeways and darkened city streets.

In each place, it has a different name.

6

WALKING IN MIST

IT FELT GREAT to be outside and moving. The morning drizzle cooled the air, but I was warm from climbing the steep and rugged fire road. My eyeglasses kept filming over with condensation. I needed the glasses for reading any tracks I might find in the loose dirt of the trail, but I had to remove them to see the broad expanses of open hills ahead of me. Eyeglasses off, now on, now off again. Continually wiping them with the blue bandanna. Every so often, when I brought the binoculars into play, the equation became even more complex. Things used to be a lot easier before I became older and needed glasses.

I decided to leave the trail entirely and to climb uphill through the damp grass toward the mountain's summit. A few deer ticks might be encountered along the way, but they could be easily found and knocked off.

Heading high across the open grassland offered me relief from having to continually look down for tracks. However, as if to compensate, as soon as I left the trail my mind began to overwork. As my visual faculties had less work to do, my thinking processes seemed to kick into high gear. And, somehow, thoughts of mountain lions obliquely led me to a consideration of the fine arts of Japan.

A century ago, a mountain lion hunter would have envisioned a pelt, a mounted head, or a tooth or claw as a valued trophy. With this kind of relic in hand, the hunter could exhibit tangible evidence of his prowess.

My wish, however, was merely to be able to *see* a mountain lion. I was not the least interested in capturing a souvenir, even on photographic film. For me, the mountain lion's elusive qualities were what gave the hunt its challenge and its merit. The animal's evanescence was one of the qualities I found most attractive.

This is where Japanese art came in. One of its most admired qualities has always been the emphasis it places on the momentary and the fleeting. This high regard for transitory nature has been exhibited time after time, in one artistic creation after another. Whether this ephemerality is portrayed in painting (rapid brush strokes on silk or paper), Noh drama or Kabuki (both being performed and disappearing in real time), or haiku poetry (quickly written words expressing a single moment), the artist's relationship to the transitory has often been paramount. Even in its architecture, traditional Japan has produced buildings not of stone or brick but of paper and wood. Artworks displayed in the home are regularly removed and replaced with other works. And the Japanese art of flower arranging, ikebana, utilizes flowers that had been cut from the soil. This rootless, isolated detachment of beauty emphasizes once again the temporary nature of the flowers. For viewers, the existence of these arrangements is made more resplendent by knowing that the plants are in the act of dying.

I stopped thinking long enough to catch my breath and noticed, beside me, a rocky knoll covered with scarlet penstemon. These wildflowers conveyed no human message, yet even without my glasses I seemed to see them clearly. There was no reason to arrange these flowers in any way other than how they were naturally presented. There was no need to move them somewhere else or contain them. They were not there for me but for themselves, and any appreciation I might have for them was secondary.

Suddenly it started to rain, and even though I hadn't yet reached the summit, I decided that I'd gone far enough. With hardly any thoughts at all, I made a steep and direct, off-trail descent—slithery and exhilarating—back to where my climb that day had started.

7

THE LANDSCAPE

I THINK BACK to when I first began to look for cougars. While working in the yard, I would often look up toward the twisted ridges of the hills and coastal mountains that surround our house. And when running errands, I would nearly drive my car off the road as I scanned the high, open hillsides while negotiating the snaky mountain thoroughfares that take us from our house to town. The high-placed groves and rocky outcrops around us were all potential shelters that might reveal the form of an animal resting during daylight. I had seen enough foxes, bobcats, and coyotes in this fashion to dare think that I might also discover a mountain lion this way as well. The chances of this happening, however, were extremely low. It was much more likely that I would put the car in a ditch all by myself, with no one else having even the faintest idea of why I had done it.

Marin County, where we live, is a wonderful place to look for something. It's a land of wilderness, parks, marine sanctuaries, farmlands, small villages, and manageably sized cities. Here one can find an abundance of wildflowers and mushrooms, along with meditation centers and ethnic restaurants. There are elephant seals, car dealerships, redwood trees, high-tech industries, rare falcons, and imprisoned felons, all sharing one of the loveliest landscapes and coastlines anywhere.

Long ago, the grizzly bear was king of our county. But, as is the case in the rest of California, this marvelous creature is currently absent. The last county sighting of a grizzly occurred back in the 1880s, but some residents here, like members of the Pacific island cargo cults, still wait hopefully for their return. It's not necessary that something actually exist here for its presence to be anticipated.

The mountain lion is now the largest and longest-established carnivore in our area. No one has any real idea how many of them are now living in the county. Park rangers, research biologists, ranchers, naturalists, and independent observers all talk in terms of "territory" and "home ranges." The range of a healthy lion might vary from a few square miles to hundreds of square miles or more. It's difficult, even impossible, to determine, especially in the dense forests and steep, labyrinthine canyons of these coastal mountains. The home range of an animal refers to the area occupied by an animal, which it regularly patrols, but which may or may not be defended against others of the same species. The area within a home range that is definitely defended constitutes the animal's "territory." A cougar can only defend its territory when it sees direct encroachment by another animal. A visiting cat can find many places in which to hide itself. Whatever a mountain lion's home range or territory consists of, the fact is that most of their movements across these lands go undetected. They are masters at remaining hidden. The corridors of their travels are unclear. Some occupy an area year-round, while others are merely passing through. Their roaming is so extensive that any census would risk counting animals more than once in areas many miles apart. A mountain lion can easily travel thirty or forty miles in a day. Without documentary photographs or radio collars, it is nearly impossible to tell one lion from another. They seem to melt into each other. They are uncannily able to make themselves invisible.

To make matters worse, some experts have estimated that as many as 85 to 90 percent of reported mountain lion sightings are erroneous. Most of these misidentifications are of bobcats, which are subject to variation in both their size and coloring, and which are much more likely to be seen by a passing mountain biker or mushroom gatherer than are the more secretive, larger felines. Coyotes, foxes, dogs, and house cats are also reported incorrectly as being cougars. Even seasoned naturalists can make mistakes when conditions are marginal or when their observations are too hurried.

California has about 90,000 square miles of cougar habitat, and Marin County offers the perfect home for a healthy resident population of mountain lions. Large areas of open space are surrounded by forested cover, scattered outcrops and promontories, scrub oak, redwood, fir, manzanita and madrone, winding creek beds, and hidden canyons. There seems to be no end to the supply of resident smaller mammals, particularly the black-tailed deer that constitute the mountain lion's major food source. And researchers tell us that these big cats have long been well established here. The cougar's ancestors have been here for over 2 million years, and the modern cougar evolved 100,000 years ago.

Statewide, the mountain lion population has been dwindling since 1996. The number of lions near Bishop, on the eastern side of the Sierra, is only one-sixth of what it was just five years ago.

8

NEW YORK CITY REPORT

INCOMPREHENSION AND MYSTERY are sometimes not very far away. Today, I am doing nothing more dangerous than reading the *New York Times* when I find an article headlined "Four Arrested in Attempt to Sell Mountain Lion." Four men in New York City have been arrested for trying to sell a six-month-old, fifty-pound female cougar to an undercover officer in Queens. They had been keeping the animal in an apartment in Harlem.

I read the report a second time while pouring myself an unneeded extra cup of coffee. I wonder where the men found the lion, how they had been able to transport it, and how they could have kept it, undetected, in a New York City apartment.

It seems clear that the pursuit of mountain lions can lead one in many different directions. Learning the answers to these New York City questions would probably be interesting and satisfying work, but the pursuit of these answers would be an obvious diversion from my plans. The real story behind this news report would be fascinating, possibly even screenplay material—the lowest of all common denominators—but this was clearly a trail for someone else to follow. If I was ever going to make headway in learning about mountain lions, I would have to continually discern the difference between the main trail and the lesser footpaths that might branch off and sidetrack me in the wrong direction.

Wild animals survive by being focused on what is before them. They live by using their innate skills and instincts, coupled with a relaxed awareness. They can concentrate on one thing while not ignoring anything else around them. These qualities are equally as necessary in the person who hopes to find one of these wild animals in open country. We must set all bewildered distraction aside. We also must confront the possibility that the thing we're looking for might be in the most unlikely and unexpected of places, even in a New York City apartment.

9

MANJUSHRI

A ZEN TEACHER once asked a student, "Who is brave enough to remove the bell that's tied around the neck of the golden-haired lion?" The answer of course was, and remains, "The one who tied it around her neck in the first place."

Manjushri, the archetypal figure representing Buddhist wisdom, is often portrayed as riding on the back of a lion. (Although it should be added that contemporary artist Mayumi Oda once depicted this figure as a rather voluptuous goddess riding on a bicycle.) The classic rendering of Manjushri always has quite a positive and formidable presence. In his left hand, he often holds a book of Buddhist teachings, and in his right, the sword of wisdom. This sword is used not to kill any living beings but to excise anger and greed, and to cut away the folly of having preconceptions.

The lion represents Manjushri's noble background and his fearlessness; and it usually appears quite relaxed and unhurried. The two beings seem totally comfortable with one another and as intimate as two close friends. Manjushri once said, "I come from nowhere, and when I disappear, I disappear into nowhere." It was as though the lion too had spoken.

THE GODS OFTEN ride exotic animals, but the rest of us must walk, or perhaps ride words. Before we developed language, we were at the mercy of all wild predatory carnivores. Wildcats, in particular, considered humans to be choice prey. Without adequate defensive weapons, our nascent ability to communicate with other human beings, and our discovery of ways to create fire, were the two factors that rescued us from being perpetually devoured.

By talking to one another, we were able to communicate our sense of danger, to exchange important ideas, and to set rough schedules for standing guard.

Words carried us from a state of fear and hysteria into a world of brotherhood, logical resolve, and reasoned calm; and words can still transport us to any distant or imagined place. Without the constant presence of the living word, we would again be consumed by our own ignorance. The lion would, once again, be invited back to the human banquet.

10

THE TRACKING CLASS

Sometimes, one must imagine even what is real.

IT IS ANOTHER radiant morning in the softly folded ridges of northern California's coastal range, and even though winter has long since passed, the bunched needles of the Bishop pines appear thickly iced by the expanding sunlight. A shining, ninety-foot-long Douglas fir lies where it has fallen among the pines, broken-backed and nearly stripped of bark by hosts of ravens and raccoons and a dozen years of hard-hitting weather. On a long, tilted section of the fir log, a mountain lion sits nonchalantly, her tawny fur glistening in the bright warmth of the early morning. Slowly she stretches, raising her hindquarters and reaching forward with her sharpened claws to her utmost limit. For a generous instant of four or five seconds, she is as frozen as a winter photograph. Then she gathers herself together, hops down from the log, and disappears.

UNFORTUNATELY for me, this imaginary photograph had never been developed. I had still not sighted one of these animals in my own home territory. Yet friends continued to report coming across them when out on walks. They had even seen them resting beneath other people's cars. On one occasion, a mountain lion needed rescuing after it got itself entangled in a set of bedsprings abandoned in the hills above our house. These lions were seemingly all about us, and yet, to me, they remained invisible. After many recent weeks of looking, I had still not seen one. I began to think of this as some kind of personal failing. Maybe I just wasn't desperate enough. An intractable sense of doubt began to descend upon me. What was I doing wrong? Why didn't these lions like me?

A few days later, in our local paper, I was surprised to find an announcement detailing the merits of an upcoming animal-tracking class. Taking this as an auspicious sign, and thinking that this class might bring me some advantage in finding a lion, I enrolled in it immediately.

THE CLASS WAS held on one of those mornings when everything seemed to be the same color, that kind of translucent hue that falls somewhere between mourning-dove gray and the faint shades of an aged and faded pencil drawing. The cars and trucks scattered throughout the parking lot seemed inordinately bright and shiny by comparison. And the walk from the parking area up through the eucalyptus and bay trees and coastal live oaks was enjoyable and restorative. Up a gentle slope, on somewhat higher ground, in a large, open area, about fifteen people were standing about, talking or sitting quietly on tree stumps beside their brightly colored day packs, bagged lunches, and coffee. It was late spring, and the air was warm and still as it surrounded this genial gathering of would-be trackers. The class instructor checked names from a list as each new person arrived, and before long the group was called together and formed into a circle, and the general layout of the day-long class was explained. The class, although small, represented a wide variety of types: housewives, teenagers, avuncular outdoorsmen, college students, and a young couple who looked as though they might chuck their business careers and become professional hunter-gatherers. The couple wore complete safari gear, including matching wide-brimmed hats with zebra-skin hat bands.

The first item on the day's agenda called for us to walk fifty yards or so to a spot where we could form a single line, all facing outward, an arm's length apart from one another, and where we could look out over a hillside expanse of grassland toward a dry creek bed and a wooded area beyond. We were instructed to look at nothing in particular, but rather to let our eyes become a bit unfocused, to let ourselves be rather "Zen-like," feeling the overview of the landscape rather than trying to pick out any of the particulars that offered themselves up to us. As I had had quite a bit of Zen training and had also neglected to arm myself with extra amounts of morning coffee, it was not difficult for me to slip into an almost trancelike state.

Later, as we reviewed field guides and tracking manuals, held exercises along popular hiking trails where tracks had been obscured by bird-watchers and baby strollers, and shared a nondenominational New Age prayer, a steady, leaden, pounding awareness began to manifest itself within me. I realized without any possibility of doubt that there was no way that this friendly collection of folks, who greatly enjoyed being together in the out-of-doors, was on this day ever going to actually see or track an animal.

It was at this point that I was seized by an almost divine inspiration. Feverishly, I began studying my classmate's footwear. It took all of my resolve and cunning not to be caught kneeling at their feet. The safari twins, of course, sported identical trekking-style boots; only the sizes were different. Many of the others wore running-type shoes—Nike, New Balance, and those brands more nondescript. One of the older, outdoor types wore badly worn work boots with very little heel. A cheery middle-aged woman wore flats. Her friend wore sandals. The instructor had on a pair of well-used hiking boots, older-style Asolos with Vibram soles.

During the lunch break, I took my pen and notebook and hiked back down to the parking area. There, on narrow, blue-lined paper, I carefully drew a plan of the arrangement of cars, pickup trucks, and vans, noting the types of vehicles, their colors, and where they were parked. Then I found a place, away from the trail, inside a small circle of young eucalyptus, where I could sit undisturbed and eat my lunch.

A few hours later, around five o'clock, after more meandering through the woods and cutting across the weeds and grasses, we met again to form our good-bye circle. Some people shook hands, a few exchanged phone numbers, and most congratulated the instructor on the wisdom and sensitivity of his instruction. As it was very late spring, the sun was still relatively high in the sky. I waited near the trail to give the others time to reach their vehicles and drive off. Then I cleaned my glasses, unpacked my notebook, and got down to serious business.

The sunlight was bright enough that I could see very well, but it was also low enough to sharpen the contrast between the ground's surface area and the darkly shadowed indentations of footprints, disturbed soils, and tumbled stones that marked the passage of each of these student trackers across the landscape. Early mornings and late afternoons are ideal tracking periods for this reason. In the midday glare of the sun, it is often easy to overlook the obvious. Things are cloaked in an even brightness, buried in an even light.

Without too much effort, using my notes on their vehicles and shoes, I soon ascertained that Flats and Sandals had immediately left the area and walked, more or less directly, down to Sandals's new Volkswagen Jetta. It had been a long day, and they were probably eager to get to their respective homes and begin preparing dinner. The instructor, Asolos with Vibrams, had waited until everyone else had gone and then driven off in a dusty Corolla. His footprints could be seen clearly overlaying all the others. Nikes #1 and Nondescript #1 had left together in a Ford pickup with an old washing machine faceup in the back. Nikes #2 was alone. She also had a VW. I probably could have won a thousand-dollar bet on what the safari twins were driving even if I had not ventured down to the parking area earlier—a Land

Rover. But it was not a new one, and an old crease in its passenger-side door harbored rust. Work Boots had an older-model Pontiac, a big car with badly worn tires, just like his boots. Many of the other prints left me more uncertain. The tracks of the older running shoes were shallow, smooth, and difficult to distinguish. One man had feet quite a bit larger than everyone else's, so I was able to follow his route down the hill and across the parking area to where another Toyota had been waiting.

This entire enterprise—the stooped walking, the taking of notes, and the climbing and reclimbing of the hillside so many times—eventually began to wear me out. And the fading light was becoming bothersome and nearly nonexistent. I walked one last time up to the place where the day's class had been held. It was indeed getting dark, and the surrounding shadows were becoming indistinguishable from one another. Soon the deer and raccoons would be foraging throughout this area. Maybe even a mountain lion would appear. Who knew? The day had started off a bit frustrating—the tracking class had been a disappointment—but I had picked up a few valuable skills this day in spite of it all. After all, I had tracked down my own tracking class and determined which vehicle carried each individual student home. And as luck would have it, standing there in that open space, upright and alone in the falling darkness, I thought I heard the footsteps of animals in the shadowed leaves off somewhere to my left.

Just as my day was ending, other creatures were only now beginning to come forth, learning things of their own, sniffing tracks, wondering about tiny, puzzling traces of evidence, questioning and trying to reconstruct the threadlike sequences of travel, and studying all possible individual detail of those who had visited and walked here earlier and what they had done on this hazy, yet brilliant, springtime day.

11

DEVIL'S GULCH

SHORTLY AFTER taking the tracking class, I went out to talk with Lanny Waggoner, the supervising ranger at one of the state parks nearby. I told him that I had come to talk about mountain lions.

In the generous spirit typical of him, he took a long time to tell me about cougar sightings in his park's jurisdiction during the past two or three years. Lots of misidentified bobcats, he said. But there was definitely an adult male cougar resident in the area. He had a "largish" head, which had been commented upon by several of those who reported seeing him. This had earned the cougar the rather undignified appellation Buckethead. There was also a smaller, female cougar, with a cub, observed in Devil's Gulch and on Mount Barnabe, two of the more popular hiking destinations within the park's boundaries. The fresh carcass of a lion-killed deer had been found just two days earlier, and it seemed to me that this might be an auspicious time to take a walk out along the Devil's Gulch trail and see what was there.

By then it was midday, and I really had no expectation of actually seeing a mountain lion. But recent rains had made finding tracks a distinct possibility.

In addition, the steady breeze coming directly toward me ensured that my scent would be carried away from the direction in which I was headed. It would also help to muffle the sound of my careful, measured walking. It seemed to me, then, that I was already on my way to behaving like a tracker.

It took a long time to walk out to the end of the gulch and back, a round-trip distance of only about two miles. Looking for tracks takes time. Cooper's hawks and red-tailed hawks kept me company while I alternated close observation of the muddy trail with glassing the vast open hillsides with my binoculars. I investigated every rock and random piece of wood for some evidence, some clue of *something*. The tracks I found were all man-made, or those of horses, deer, or raccoons. The hillsides held a few resting raptors, and I could see a dozen dairy cows high on the misty northern ridges. There would be no cougars today.

I walked back to the horse corrals, nearly returning to where I'd started. I tried to scrape the mud from my boots as I looked at the bulletin board the park rangers had placed beside the trail. A large, laminated informational brochure offered general facts concerning mountain lions and told hikers what to do in the event of an encounter. (Don't run! Stand your ground! Try to make yourself appear as large as possible! Make noise!) As I was looking this over, I began to experience a rather strange sensation—a feeling that I, myself, was being watched. I turned slowly to my right, and my heart began pounding excitedly as I saw the large feline face that studied me. The animal lay in the grass, only about sixty feet away. It seemed too small to be a lion, but could it perhaps be the cub? I slowly raised the field glasses up to my eyes and somehow fumbled them into focus. The expression on the bobcat's face was quite complex. It seemed to include friendship, contempt, bewilderment, disinterest, understanding, and merry amusement all at once. I watched it for ten minutes, then walked back to my car, got in the driver's seat, thought for a moment about filing a spurious mountain-lion-sighting report, shook my head, and headed home.

Later that day I dug out all of the county maps that I had stashed away, maps that included the Golden Gate National Recreation Area, Mount Tamalpais State Park, Muir Woods National Monument, the Marin Municipal Water District lands, Samuel P. Taylor State Park, Tomales Bay State Park, and the Point Reyes National Seashore. I found an unused 200-page school notebook and a new ballpoint pen. I cleaned up my boots and located my Swiss army knife and the stainless steel bottle I use for carrying coffee. Then, slowly and carefully, I began polishing the lenses of my trusty binoculars.

Somewhere out there, I felt certain, in the hills and canyons depicted within these folded maps, a secret and bewhiskered presence was waiting for me to find it.

THE MAPS, notebook, and binoculars were in their own way symbolic. They could be looked upon as representing two radically different approaches to learning. One of these roads led toward research; note-taking, the library, the Internet, and interviews with dozens of people. Numbers could be compiled, data gathered, facts checked, and book and magazine articles and newspaper files pulled from their resting places. Reason, organization, and ingenuity would be called for.

The second of these two paths would be much less exact. It would call upon powers of direct observation, on the development of little-used instincts, and on perseverance and good fortune. The binoculars would help bring things closer, but the other tools would only aid me in trying to understand what it was I might be seeing.

Most of what we learn comes from outside our own personal experience. We trust what people tell us, what we read, and what we see on television. A large percentage of our lives is composed of this secondhand information. Even our thinking and intellectualizing can interfere with our own life experience. This is why Zen teachers stop their students cold when they begin to theorize. And it was one of the main reasons I had begun my search.

When we walk through an urban neighborhood, all of our senses are at work; we see the shop windows, hear the motorcycle, smell the garlic sizzling in the restaurant kitchen and the exhaust of the passing bus. Our memory cells receive and store this information, and it becomes part of us. If we are searching for something, in a city or in the country, our senses become even more sharply defined. Hunters, poets, birders, graduate students, mining engineers, and astronomers all offer examples of this kind of focused activity. History instructs us that wonderful things are much more likely to occur to those who remain alert and look at things carefully.

In nature, the signs we look for are sometimes difficult to see, even when they are directly in our path.

As the poet Gary Snyder said so well, "Beyond all this studying and managing and calculating, there's another level to nature. You can go about learning the names of things and doing inventories of trees, bushes, and flowers. But nature often just flits by and is not easily seen in a hard, clear light. Our actual experience of many birds and wildlife is chancy and quick. Wildlife is known as a call, a cough in the dark, a shadow in the shrubs. You can watch a cougar on a wildlife video for hours, but the real cougar shows herself only once or twice in a lifetime. One must be tuned to hints and nuances."

After more than thirty years of living in the foothills of the Sierra Nevada and spending a great deal of that time out-of-doors, Snyder has seen the mountain lion on just a few occasions. One of these sightings was most unusual. Gary had been visiting a neighbor and was walking down from the nearby ridge to his home when he observed a cougar sitting near one of the windows of the house. The animal appeared to be listening intently as one of Snyder's stepdaughters practiced the piano.

Part of the delight in looking for something is in not knowing when it might turn up. Clearly, the cougar is an animal that lives by its own rules and laws; it follows its own whims and caprices, and it has its own necessities for survival. The mountain lion is a creature impossible to anticipate. And it's interesting to think that, once in a while, one of them might like to listen to the sounds of a piano being played.

12

RETURN

A WEEK OR so later, I went out to the Devil's Gulch trail again. The rains were over, and the sky was sunny blue. The puddled ruts in the trail reflected oak, bay, and fir, along with newly greened grasses and remnants of the dead and desiccated weeds of the previous summer. The bobcat was no longer there. This, of course, was no surprise, but it started me smiling as I recalled another incident here in the park the summer before. A man had reported being chased by a mountain lion. The man had run into a park restroom, where he remained until five-thirty in the morning. At this time, he felt that it was "safe enough to leave." The rangers who received the report were skeptical. They informed the man that there was "a very large bobcat that lives in Devil's Gulch," and pointed out that bobcat attacks on human beings were rare, if not nonexistent. To their knowledge, there had never been a report of a bobcat attacking a person in California.

I couldn't help wondering whether the animal I'd seen a few days earlier could have been the culprit in this case. The man involved was simply victimized by his own ignorance, something we all occasionally come to experience.

I found my own encounter with the bobcat heartening. While scanning the mountainsides for cougars, I had been guilty of wishful thinking. Along with missing many of the things that were right in front of me, I had also seen things that were not truly there. I had seen a dozen illusive cougars on these hillsides that were fabricated of stones, shrubs, shadows, turkey vultures, even fence posts. Not a true mountain lion among them. I felt muddleheaded for having been so easily and thoroughly deceived. I should have remembered that Einstein once said, "Nature conceals her secrets because she is sublime, not because she is a trickster." We, ourselves, are often the ones who are easiest to fool.

But the bobcat had been genuine. His grin had not been imaginary. He was not silkscreened or composed of pixels. He had relaxed in the grass and watched me, even as I was watching him. I wanted to think of this animal as a friend, but this was truly a silly and preposterous thing to hope for. It would have to be enough just realizing that we were both out there together at the same time, enjoying the sunshine, walking around, checking things out, all by ourselves. What was the bobcat looking for? I wondered. But having no real way of answering this, I put away my binoculars and turned once again toward home.

13

ZEN TEACHERS AND WORDS

MANY ZEN TEACHERS have cautioned their students against any dependence upon words, either written or spoken. They have likened words to thorns and briars, and compared having an idle conversation to taking a walk through wild thistles and entangling vines. At the very least, we are told, we should give careful attention to what we say. This should be true at all times, but particularly so when we purport to speak the dharma, the real truth of things. When we speak to others with the intention of relaying or explaining Buddhist truths, we soon learn just how many traps and snares there are; and we learn the clever ways in which they can lie in wait, ready to spring upon us at the first sign of unsteadiness or hesitation. That we can be ambushed by our own words is one of the great lessons of Buddhism, and it is a lesson we learn constantly.

Sometimes we must look beyond the physical objects we find in front of us. We must look at what we hear and watch what we might say. The Tang dynasty Zen master Tokusan once addressed a group of his monks, urging them to say something relevant without using either words or silence. When a monk stepped forward and began to bow, Tokusan struck him. Bewildered, the monk complained, "Why am I struck before I have even had a chance to speak?" Tokusan replied, "If I had waited for you to say something, it would have already been too late." A later teacher put it differently. He simply said, "We must see the lightning before we hear the thunder."

To say something relevant is to avoid the obvious and to resist the impulse to impress others. It is to downplay one's natural abilities for oration. Whenever we are asked to provide an answer to another person's burning question, we would do well to weigh our thoughts carefully. There are some questions whose true destiny is to remain always a question. When we give voice to an answer, any answer, our first word may already be too late.

But where does this leave us? Do we, in order to

stay on the path and avoid these off-trail encounters with entangling weeds, remain always silent, afraid to move ahead or ever to speak our thoughts? Of course not. The Zen teacher's cautions are directed not against our ever using words but against our *dependence* upon them; and we are advised to choose our words well. To find the answers to all our burning questions may not be what's most important. Sometimes, the teachers say, to determine just one adequate word is to find the lion that hides behind a single blade of grass.

14

THE LIBRARY

THE UNSETTLED NATURE of my days has been somewhat eased by the return of winter rains. However, during the heaviest downpours, our house nearly becomes an ark. Runoff streams down the hillsides above us, seeps in under the foundation, and comes to rest beneath the hardwood floor of our bedroom. In the middle of the night, raccoons invade the crawl space under the house, chittering and splashing like children attending a pool party. Being an insomniac, and an infrequent swimmer, I find this unbounded merriment to be impudent and highly irritating.

The uninsulated house is quiet during the daytime, but in the rainy season it is perpetually damp. Its interior winter temperatures are often colder than those of the circulating air outside. When the weather's nice, I go out walking; but when it rains torrentially or gets too cold, I head for the library. It's warm and dry there, and I can work on research or write while avoiding the effects of winter weather. One rainy day, I read about Sam Spade trying to find the Maltese Falcon. I take solace in learning that even fictional detectives can spend their time looking for something they don't understand.

When skies are clear, I tackle the mountain trails again, looking for cat tracks. I am a private eye involved in a hot case, slogging through mud in search of the holy grail, learning how one clue often belies another, how vagaries interpose themselves between the seeker and the thing sought.

15

RAVENS

AFTER THE MOST recent rainstorm, a robin lands heavily on a pine bough, knocking loose more rain. Overhead, the constant, raucous call of ravens almost brings a sympathetic rawness to my own throat. The birds are roosted high, and are querulous and unsettled due to my seated presence beneath them. I've been sitting here for nearly a half hour, scanning the hillsides for anything that might move. Unfortunately, not much is stirring. Once in a while, a periodic breeze rustles the scattered patches of damp grass along the edges of the trail.

A friend saw a cougar here just two days ago. I wonder now whether any lion in the vicinity would be repelled or attracted by the clamor coming from above. The raven's rattling is almost metallic; so insistent and insinuating that I decide to move up to a higher elevation.

Once out on the sunlit crest of the hill, I suddenly realize that there's little hope of spotting a lion today. The active mode of these animals is so highly pitched that they require great periods of rest. While deer and other herbivores spend most of their time eating, lions sleep. They are usually active for only a few hours each day, and even then they strive to stay concealed.

Often, when I'm out rambling the hillsides, I come upon small herds of feeding deer. Ordinarily, I pay them little notice. My eyes are drawn to the vantage points above them and to the rocks and brush near where they graze. Chances of finding a lurking cougar this way are slim, but one must entertain every possibility.

My friend had been exceedingly lucky, and this good fortune had probably occurred because she couldn't have cared less whether she saw a mountain lion or not. She had taken a good look at the lion, and the lion had looked at her. And then, quickly, the lion had jumped away.

This appears so starkly elementary as not to merit comment. It is not at all the story of someone engaged in a vision quest. My friend had shown up at the right time, and so had the cougar. Nothing could have been simpler. So why am I made to spend all this time looking? The mountain lion is certainly miles away by now. And I am left here with only the scolding ravens and the enticing hula of a patch of rip-gut grass that might still hold the mountain lion's scent.

16

EAGLES

WE CAN NEVER predict when the wild side of life will present itself to us. I remember one afternoon when I walked from a heavily forested coastal trail onto a rain-slicked beach of small stones. Just a few yards from me, slightly farther out, a pair of resting bald eagles sat undisturbed, bedraggled and forlorn-looking, hunched right down in the tidal-flat mud. I stood motionless and soon lost all sense of time. I had the feeling that I was really seeing eagles for the first time ever; exposed there in the soaking rain, I felt that the birds and I were sharing something immediate. By not flying away, they seemed to offer me a quiet entrance into their lives. Beneath this expansive canopy of loosened clouds and cold water, a true feeling of intimacy was created. For maybe fifteen minutes nothing happened. It was just rain and the eagles and me. There was not one second out of this quarter hour that did not resonate with life. Only later did my thinking and conjecture make their appearance, and they added nothing to the event itself.

The things I pursued in the past had often seemed to be driven away. When I relaxed, interesting things sometimes happened. This was how I had discovered the eagles. It was all part of learning, and of occasionally giving things up to chance. Looking for a mountain lion, and believing that there might be value in such a pursuit, might appear to some as unorthodox or eccentric. It's not the kind of activity that ranks highly on most people's lists of things to do. But if nothing else, it puts a person out near the living edge of things, on foreign soil, where the air is a bit rarefied and where a rebirth of the senses is possible. It's a place of unfamiliar patterns, held together with thinly twisted wiring and fuzzy logic, where quick and sometimes baffling encounters with nature can bring new possibilities, either ridiculous or meaningful.

17

SEKKO AND THE DRAGON

ON THE WALL above my writing desk is a card that says, "Do not be amazed at the true dragon." This old Zen saying is based in part on a centuries-old story concerning a man named Sekko, who was inordinately fond of dragons. He collected paintings, small sculptures, and assorted household implements, all featuring the images and likenesses of dragons. He even began to create his own renderings of dragons, and soon his house was filled with every type of dragon imaginable. One day a real dragon heard about the man Sekko, who had such friendly feelings toward his kind, and decided that it might be nice to pay him a visit. When Sekko saw the dragon looking in at him through the window, he fainted and fell to the floor unconscious. After he had revived, he looked again at the now-vacated window and felt totally disoriented. He hadn't recognized this strange new animal that had peered in on him. He was sure he had never seen one before, and he had no idea what it was.

That message on my wall had always seemed good advice for writers. It cautioned against closed-mindedness and offered a warning against forming conclusions too soon. It suggested, also, that we try not to become jaded, that we never lose our own capacity for being invigorated by surprise.

In many respects, mountain lions are no less mythical than dragons, and certainly they are just as subtle and mercurial in their ways. Scientists disagree as to where they may have originated. Surprisingly, at least some evidence (based on DNA analysis) contends that the cougar's closest modern relative might be the African cheetah. This makes more sense when we realize that there were at least two types of cheetah once resident in the Americas. Still, many biologists discount this theory. The controversy over the cougar's origin and the lack of agreement on what it should be called are both overshadowed by the fact that there is clearly no commonly held viewpoint concerning the mountain lion's standing in the world today. It is defined, variously, as a predatory carnivore, a ghost, a pest, a totem, a symbol of wilderness, and a pain in the neck for the ranching and agricultural communities. It evokes very strong responses in those who are otherwise hesitant to speak about such things. It engenders a wide array of feelings ranging from fear and hatred to friendship, protection, and curiosity. Like Sekko's dragons, there seems to be no end to the variety of forms this particular creature can take.

On the wall opposite the dragon card is a rather cluttered Buddhist altar. Shrines such as this have nothing to do with worship but are more correctly viewed as a kind of visual reminder, a spiritual Post-it note to help keep us on the proper path. This particular signpost today consists of a makeshift collection of both the spiritual and the casually mundane. There is a small statue of Kannon, the bodhisattva of compassion. And there are scattered sticks of incense, some ballpoint pens, a pocket knife, a pinecone, and a few smooth stones. There are also two items that almost defy description. They closely resemble partially melted scoops of vanilla ice cream that have tumbled from their cones onto sand. These are plaster casts of the tracks once made by a mountain lion.

These particular tracks are not a whole lot larger than those of a German shepherd, but they differ in several respects. The subtle differences are what one looks for first when out searching in the field. First of all, the prints of the cat are rounder; not quite circular, but more so than in the elliptical print of the canine. Usually, but not always, there are no claw marks in the tracks of cats. Unlike a dog's claws, those of a cat are commonly retracted into protective sheaths when not used. Also, the imprinted shape of the animal's heel pads differs considerably in dogs and cats. And a cat's toes are less symmetrically arranged.

Wherever you travel, it is much more likely that you'll find tracks of animals other than mountain lions. Looking for lion tracks has been compared to seeking stars in the daylight. To cast prints like these in plaster is to try to catch something ephemeral and to halt its transitory nature. Placing these relics on an altar is a way of bringing something temporary— two isolated tracks made in gritty dust—back onto the path itself.

18

SERPENTS

ONE SUMMER long ago, I was working on a ranch near California's northern border, cleaning out a corral that held two mares with young foals, when the horses began dancing around nervously, showing signs of fear. A rattlesnake was crawling slowly toward them across the open ground. Without thinking, I followed my first instinct and beheaded the snake with the shovel I was holding. After just a few seconds, the decapitated body of the snake began to crawl away. I tapped its rattle with the handle of the shovel, and was amazed to see the headless snake coil instantly and face me, perfectly ready to strike. Even without a brain, the rattlesnake's body was still fully prepared, for a time, to defend itself; and a moment later its dying heart led it back toward the wild grasses from where it had come.

In that moment, it was as if my own ignorance had been struck a blow. Until then, I had always believed that all conscious thought and determination originated in the mind. I had never seen a clearer refutation of this rule. The snake had no mind, but it had something else to guide it.

These insightful moments of wildness are often rare in our lives, almost nonexistent when we live in cities dedicated to preventing any unbidden frontal attack from natural forces. In large urban communities, encounters with wildness are mostly limited to chance sightings of mice, pigeons, thunderclouds, or the greenish mold growing on last week's bread. To meet with a mountain lion or a rattlesnake would be unthinkable.

Yet every so often these things turn up in our lives anyway; a bewildered cougar emerges near a shopping mall, or a black bear cub makes an exploratory trek across a schoolyard. Nature is anything but predictable, and our newspapers often report the folly and risk of our becoming too complacent.

When I was working on the ranch in northern California, we had a neighbor who kept a sawed-off shotgun, filled with buckshot, behind the folding seat of his old pickup. This weapon was used exclusively on snakes, for which our neighbor had an avenging hatred. The rattlesnakes in that area were particularly ill-tempered in early spring and would sometimes strike at the tires of our vehicles as we drove slowly along the dirt roads. Whenever our neighbor spotted one, he would pull his truck over, set the hand brake, and after a few steps, blow the snake to pieces. He had once carried his early-morning coffee out to this same pickup truck and found a rattler sleeping on the seat, behind the steering wheel. He told me that he'd hated them ever since, and that fragmented rattlesnake meat emitted a fragrance much like that of cucumber.

My own encounters with rattlesnakes have become a great deal less violent. I remember once hiking with my wife on a mountain we'd never visited before when I stopped short, overcome by a sudden concern as to the possibility of snakes. The surrounding habitat was the ideal environment for them, and as the trail was narrow and only permitted us to walk single file, I suggested in stereotypically manly fashion that it might be better if I led the way.

After no more than twenty steps, I felt a clutching feeling at my throat. It wasn't fear. My wife had grabbed me by the back of my shirt collar and pulled me backward, preventing me from stepping directly on a coiled rattlesnake that I hadn't seen basking on the trail. The snake's color patterns blended perfectly with those of the uneven trail, and the reptile was coiled so tightly that it could have easily been covered by a dinner plate. I had failed to see it even though it was right out in the open, squarely in front of me. As macho guide and naturalist, I plainly had things to learn.

On another occasion, the two of us were walking along the mountain ridge behind our house; it was very late on an August afternoon, and we were on a trail we'd both hiked many times before. We found an interesting chunk of scat lying near the rocky bank that bordered the fire road. It almost certainly was that of a mountain lion; long, large in diameter, deeply segmented, filled with matted deer hair and dark with fresh blood, it resembled nothing so much as a woman's discarded braid.

We were sitting on a flat-topped boulder next to the lion sign when my wife saw a rattlesnake moving quietly past us, cutting through the crisp summer grass. That the rock we rested on was serpentine, and that the grass was *Briza maxima,* rattlesnake grass, were two additional and subtle ironies. The snake moved so peacefully that we decided to follow it for as long as we could. This was not difficult if we kept our eyes constantly on its moving body. To look away, even for a moment, would have risked losing sight of it forever against the wildly variegated background. It moved quite deliberately, and we followed it, stepping as lightly as possible, trying not to send forth any vibrations that might alarm it. We trailed it for a good ways as it wound its way carefully through the weeds and grasses and around stones and sun-hardened trunks of manzanita.

Finally it entered a partially collapsed badger hole, and our game ended. It had been strangely satisfying to follow along behind this creature, at such an unhurried pace and with no goal in mind, just to watch it move and see where it would go. The snake's demeanor had provided us with a kind of calm leadership, a relaxed guidance with no hint of threat.

As we walked down from the ridgetop that day, I thought back to the summer I had killed the snake so many years ago. It is often strange the way things occur. My feelings regarding these animals had certainly changed a great deal in the intervening years, and I wondered whether these feelings had to do merely with my growing older. When I had beheaded the snake in the center of that old corral, I had been thinking only of protecting the horses. Yet it seemed to me now that my actions had been brash and without any real consideration. I had been a young man and was full of summer, but I believed now that I had acted foolishly. After killing it, I had taken its skin, hoping to decorate my battered Stetson with the trophy of a rattlesnake-skin hatband. I nailed one end of the long skin to a large willow, where I hoped it would dry in the wind. I finished a few chores and then returned to discover that the trophy was gone.

High above me, a raven flew with the captured streamer trailing behind it. It reminded me of those airplanes that carry long banners of advertising behind them as they fly over crowded sporting events and county fairs. I wondered if this joyous flyer was carrying a particular message meant only for me.

19

THE FOURTH OF JULY

IT WAS July 4, and the little town where we live was holding its annual Independence Day parade. There were American flags and sheets of bunting, children dressed as salmon, rock bands on flatbed trucks, snare drums and sirens, fire trucks, motorcycles, bikes, horses, and a half-dozen or more ubiquitous dogs. I slowly walked the entire parade route, totally naked. I knew that I had become a mountain lion. There was no one there who could see me.

We know so little about our dreams. The mind that creates images while we sleep is the same mind that tries to analyze them after we awaken. Is this possible, or is it expecting too much? Is it like a broken tool trying to fix itself? If we were born blind, what sort of night images might we have? Would there be any difference between our dream images and those conscious perceptions we experience during the daytime? And if there *are* differences, is it really of any importance to be aware of this fact? Dreams, after all, come and go. Their transitory nature may ensure their neutrality, making them neither beneficial nor harmful to any great extent. If they serve any real purpose, perhaps that purpose does not need to be spoken of. And if there is no real purpose to our dreaming, then all of this is unnecessary conjecture to begin with.

Daydreams are another matter. These most often concern subjects we *choose* to deal with, and for this reason they are most often pleasant in nature. A fearful or paranoiac fantasy would go beyond the boundaries of the daydream, and might indicate that some other course of interpretation is called for, or that a deeper-running problem might need addressing.

But simple daydreams tell us much about ourselves: our fervent wishes, our need to escape the present, the extreme limits of imagination and creative thought. All these things are made evident in the images we gather and bring to ourselves whenever we allow our working mind to drift away, beyond the strictures of our control.

To understand our dreams may not be all that necessary, but to acknowledge our unspoken wishes may be vitally important.

A Zen teacher once asked a group of students, "What will you do after you are enlightened?" One student said that, if enlightened, he would travel all over the world and try to help others. Another student spoke of her wish to work with disabled children. The teacher said, "Then why don't you pretend that you've already achieved enlightenment and go do these things? Why don't you forget about 'enlightenment' and go make yourselves useful?"

The teacher could have said the same thing about looking for a cougar. He could have said, "Why don't you just pretend you've seen it, and go on about your life?"

There were times, of course, when this was tempting to me. If I couldn't even articulate the reasons for my search in a somewhat direct manner, why not simply make up the lie? Why not take myself off the hook I'd placed myself upon and move on to other things? Why not feign success and attempt something more meaningful?

These questions seemed to be suspended in the air. And they appeared more noticeable to me whenever I was tired. I knew that, even in half-jest, I could not pretend to have done something that I had not. To lie about finding a cougar was no less unthinkable than to claim to have caught sight of a griffin or a unicorn. This kind of deception, even when it's self-deception, and even when it's self-mocking, can only get worse. An announcement of having discovered a whole new menagerie would probably have come next.

Besides, I was enjoying the hunt. It gave me a sense of purpose, and I was becoming better at it. Already, in my eyes, I had progressed from being a tracker with no abilities to being one slightly better. At times even a moderate talent is enough to move us forward.

20

AN ENCOUNTER

MOUNT TAMALPAIS is not a particularly high mountain. It has an elevation of 2,571 feet; and if you could pile ten of these mountains on top of one another, the summit would still not reach the height of certain Himalayan peaks.

Still, it has a commanding view of the San Francisco Bay Area, and for centuries it has been a popular destination for hikers seeking a new perspective.

From the summit of Mount Tam (as it is called local-ly), one can see the bay, the breaking lines of the Pacific coast, the East Bay cities of Oakland and Berkeley, San Francisco, the cities and towns of Marin County, Lake Lagunitas, and the wilder, unin-corporated areas leading all the way north to the wine country.

The mountain's flanks are blanketed in manzanita and chamise, with gullies and canyons filled with bay laurel, live oak, monkey flower, and madrone. It has been estimated that the mountain hosts approxi-mately eight hundred different plant species. This is perfect cover for a wide variety of animals to enter and make their home.

About halfway up the mountain is a fire station, the Throckmorton Ridge division of the Marin County Fire Department. And here, on this particu-lar day, a posted notice warns hikers of a mountain lion seen in this vicinity just days earlier. This is the kind of thing you try not to forget whenever you hike alone. The possibility of a surprise encounter with a carnivore is what separates walking in bear or lion country from walking in more cultivated places.

It has been known for centuries that cougars fol-low people. Anyone who has done a great deal of hiking or bicycling in lion country has probably been within a hundred yards of a wild cougar. As long as the lion feels well enough concealed, it will not chance to show itself. But strange things some-times happen.

In a state park south of here, a man took his cam-era and a pair of binoculars and went out for a walk. As the trail he was taking was quite steep, he paused at one point during the ascent to catch his breath and to take in the surrounding view. The view to his rear included a mountain lion standing rather close behind him on the trail. This man, whose name was Tony Chiodo, then did the exact opposite of what one is supposed to do. He dropped to his knees. Cougar experts everywhere caution us that, when in a situation similar to Tony's, we should stand tall, make ourselves appear as large as possible, make a lot of noise, wave our arms, etc. Under no circumstance should we either turn and run or sit down. But Tony sat down; and the lion sat down too. Tony spoke to the animal casually as he attempted to take its photograph. The cougar was too close to be clearly seen through the camera's telephoto lens, so Tony removed the lens as he spoke, and twisted and snapped a new one into place. The lion, ignoring this awkward activity, decided to lie down, apparently quite content. After many photographs and several minutes of resting there together, Tony and the lion both stood. The lion began to walk away, and the man carefully began to follow. At that point, the cougar turned its head and emitted a short growl. Tony stopped, and the mountain lion almost immediately disappeared. A binder in the state park office contains the photographic record of this odd encounter.

An event such as this one, or one with a more violent ending, are both extreme and unlikely to occur. They are so rare as to make statistics useless. Still, they do happen. One wonders how close to an experience such as this *we* may have come at some point; how near to something truly extraordinary we may have almost stumbled.

As I continued following the trail up above the firehouse, I thought of how fortunate Tony had been to meet with such a lion. On that day, against whatever kind of odds, things had worked out well for both.

21

THE HISTORY OF CATS

IN PERU, six miles from Cuzco, there is an ancient Incan fortress named Sacsahuaman, which was designed and built in the shape of a cougar's jaws. Whereas human beings have only occupied the Americas for the past nineteen thousand years or so, the earth's carnivores evolved from a common ancestor that lived 56 million years ago. The first cats probably appeared about 37 million years ago. The fossil record goes back more than 36 million years, and it includes at least fifty different cat species. The earliest of the known cats was *Proailurus*, "early cat." About the same size as the present-day bobcat, it had a long tail and narrow limbs. All cats have a light but strong skeleton with an impressive network of heavy muscles. Cats and humans have about the same number of bones in their bodies; however, our limbs are proportionately longer by comparison, and our backbone is shorter and much more rigid. We have, as you may have already suspected, no tail.

Domestic cats have been sharing our homes for the past four thousand years. One-third of U.S. households have at least one feline resident. House cats in the United States are estimated to number somewhere close to 60 million.

Based on research and DNA analysis, thirty-six

species of wildcats are currently thought to live on Earth. These cats are classified into three groups: big cats, Old World small cats, and New World small cats. Whereas the Old World and New World cats are defined geographically, the line between big cats and small ones is often blurry. Mountain lions, leopards, and jaguars (all "medium" in size) are often included with the big cats; however, cougars are considered by some to be large members of the small cat family. Even here, there is controversy.

The forest-dwelling cats (such as jaguar and clouded leopard) have shorter, stockier limbs than some other cats. This is helpful in climbing trees and ambushing prey. The ocelot, a small forest dweller, is extremely agile, almost monkeylike, when climbing trees.

Most cats are solitary ambush hunters. Two savanna dwellers, the African lion and the cheetah, are exceptions. Both of these species hunt cooperatively with their own kind. The cheetah may be the world's finest coursing predator. It possesses a perfect combination of speed and agility. Its shoulder blades are not connected to its spine; it has no collar bone; its enlarged heart and lungs quickly process blood and oxygen. From a standing start, with a stride longer than that of a racehorse, it can reach speeds of nearly seventy miles an hour in seconds. If a cheetah runs for more than thirty seconds, there is the real possibility that it will overheat and die.

22

MOUNTAIN LION ANATOMY

WHEREAS THE cheetah is a specialist, the cougar is a generalist. When human beings first crossed the land bridge from Asia to North America, forty thousand years ago, cougars were already here. From that time until now, they have proven themselves ingenious at adapting and surviving on their own.

A female mountain lion can give birth at any time of year. She may have from one to six cubs (or kittens), although a litter of two or three is most common. The mother has eight mammary glands, of which six are functional. The young are born spotted. Their eyes open after about ten days and are bright blue in color. The cubs are usually weaned by two to three months. The mother will nurture her young up to eighteen months. Their spots gradually fade away, and the color of their eyes changes from blue to brownish greenish gold.

A two year old mountain lion is equivalent to a teenage human. By this time the young lion is no longer dependent on its mother, and may go looking for its own home range. These lions are known as "transients." A lion's home range averages between twenty-five and three hundred square miles, depending on the terrain and the availability of food. The home ranges of males are often larger, and usually overlap or encompass several female ranges. Females tend to have smaller ranges, in part to accommodate the raising of offspring. Mountain lions occupy a wide variety of habitats, from open deserts to alpine heights. Masters of concealment, they use any kind of cover available and have a penchant for staying low and hiding behind objects of any size.

The adult mountain lion is tawny or gray-brown in color, and whitish underneath. The tip of its tail is umber; the sides of its cheeks and the backs of its ears are often darkened. Black cougars (melanistic), though rare, have been sighted. Pure white mountain lions (albinistic) are even rarer, but are known to occur.

The cats average twenty-four to thirty-two inches in height at the shoulders, and six to eight feet in total length. They have rounded ears on a rather small head. Their long tail, a key identifying feature, can be from thirty to thirty-six inches long. Males are most often larger and heavier than females. Females usually weigh from eighty to one hundred pounds or more, while healthy, well-fed males can sometimes reach a weight of two hundred pounds.

The lion's sense of smell is much better than that of a human, but not nearly as good as a dog's. Its eyesight (including night vision) and its hearing are both highly developed.

The mountain lion has thirty teeth. Its long canines and shearing carnassials are designed to kill prey and shred flesh. A true carnivore, it takes no nourishment from sources other than meat. Its chief prey is usually deer, but it will also take rabbits, mice, squirrels, birds, and other animals when available. After killing a deer, a cougar will eat the heart, lungs, and liver first (these organs are most nutritious), and then the rear quarters and muscles of the legs. The stomach and intestines are neatly removed but rarely eaten. They are usually placed to one side, and often covered with soil, pine needles, or leaf litter. It is estimated that an adult mountain lion consumes about one deer every five to seven days. In captivity, a cougar will eat three to four pounds of food each day.

A mountain lion is about 85 percent muscle. Although not as fast as a cheetah, it can still run forty to fifty miles per hour for short distances. Before a cougar springs, it crouches, stretching its leg muscles and tendons like a rubber band storing energy. This is known as "slingshot propulsion" and enables the cat to make tremendous leaps. No one really knows how far or how high a mountain lion can jump, but leaps as long as forty-five feet and as high as fifteen feet have been recorded.

The African lion is known for its roar, but it cannot purr. A cougar can purr and snarl and scream and growl, but it cannot roar; it is the largest of the world's purring cats.

The mountain lion is attracted to catnip.

23

WALKING THROUGH GRASS, FINDING A FOX

I AM RESTING for a moment near the stock pond of a local ranch. There's a great blue heron across from me. Its legs make parallel shadows like railroad tracks across the water. Where the legs end, two birds appear to float in space, but only one of these is real.

Earlier today, I took a casual walk above the canyon. The wind scouring the hillside grasses reminded me of someone blowing on a cat's fur. It was a study in sudden shifting, an object lesson in "the winds of change."

There is a condition called peripeteia that describes any sudden change of events, any unexpected change in trajectory. This is what had happened to Tony that day, when he went out hiking and ended up sitting next to a mountain lion for nearly an hour.

The Zen master Dogen said, "Form and substance are like dew on the grass. Destiny is like a dart of lightning—emptied in an instant, vanished in a flash." As I watched the windblown grass, it was like staring downward into a roiling sea. Gazing steadily and unblinkingly at an object in constant motion will sometimes produce a feeling of relaxation, or even heightened awareness. But this time, it gave me only vertigo.

I looked up from the moving grass just in time to see a gray fox walking along the ridge above me. I had always considered these animals to be bearers of exceptional qualities; compactness, power, delicateness, all grizzled in a covering of pewter and rust and graced with wary intelligence. To see a fox abroad in daylight was not unknown, but it was rare enough to give the incident significance. Even as the animal was disappearing over the edge of the ridge, I was already running up to where it had stood. Certainly there would be no sight of it when I reached the top.

But I was wrong. The fox stood, just yards away, looking at me. I waited for a long while and then took a cautious step forward. The fox took a step away. After another pause, I took one more quiet step. The fox stepped backward once again. Our eyes were locked together, and we stepped like a couple dancing a distanced pas de deux. We alternated another step together, and I was beginning to feel amazed. One more cautious step forward, however, and my partner waved her tail and ran. I had to sit down in the grass for a while to recover.

Destiny is like a dart of lightning. The fox ran all the way down the hill, which was her destiny; and I sat there in awe, four steps down from the top, which was my destiny. The grass, unconcerned with such things as dancing or fate, just lived its life. It fulfilled its own destiny even as it was being blown about, this way and that.

BEING THAT CLOSE to a fox had been a great experience. It was one of those uncommon events that was made even more rare by its perfect spontaneity. When I first began taking these walks, on the chance that I might stumble across signs of a cougar, I had hoped to see other wildlife as well; but to predict these encounters was unthinkable, and to stand so close to a wild fox was something beyond my imagination. Interacting this way with another species, in a form of light and unpremeditated play, was enough to keep me outdoors and searching for months to come. It was the kind of interaction that made the frustrating days worthwhile. It was what kept a person looking, even when many of the motives were still unclear.

THE RABBIT AND THE STUMP

ZEN TEACHERS urge their students onward by suggesting a dedicated and energetic practice, but they also caution strongly against harboring eagerness or expectation. To chase after any special goal or outcome, they say, would be like chasing after a mad housefly in the out-of-doors. One must awaken at the perfect moment. One must ripen like a pear.

Patience, however, has its limits. It can be examined and practiced for any number of years, but it still remains finite. As the aerialist Karl Wallenda once said, "To be alive is to walk on the wire. Everything else is just waiting."

There are two basic ways of making a discovery. You can go out looking for something, or you can wait until the something comes to you. These two methods of achievement are what define the two great categories of predators, those who course or chase, and those who wait in ambush. The coursing predators include wolves, falcons, sharks, dragonflies, and cheetahs. Ambush predators are animals such as crocodiles, frogs, herons, cougars, morays, and rattlesnakes. The cougar is not built for long-range pursuit. When hunting deer, it depends upon patience, silence, surprise, and great attack strength.

Human hunters can also be categorized this way; "still hunters" (who wait in ambush) and trackers (who take action, with dogs or otherwise, in running down their prey). One must always decide beforehand which method will work best.

I had seen the fox without any intention to do so.

I had, in fact, been staring almost unconsciously at nothing more than a patch of grass when the animal appeared. I wondered if I would ever find a mountain lion in this manner. I could spend my time just walking around, staring down at grass. I could wait.

There's an old Buddhist story about a man who hunted rabbits. One day when he was out in the woods, a rabbit ran past him and collided with a tree stump, knocking itself unconscious. The man couldn't believe his own good fortune. He put the rabbit into his hunting sack. And every day, for the rest of his life, he came and watched the stump, waiting for this to happen again.

25

SHIKI

THE HAIKU POEM has been thought, by some, to be Japan's supreme contribution to world culture. These short poems—three lines, with a total of seventeen syllables—are the ultimate vehicles for describing a singular moment in nature. A classic haiku poem has never been written about lions or cougars, because these animals are only found far from Japan. The man most credited with bringing haiku into the modern era, Masaoka Shiki, thought about these foreign animals, however. Shiki, who lived from 1867 to 1902, and who was confined to bed with tuberculosis for much of his short life, once said that there were three things he'd like to see before he died: a motion picture, a bicycle race, and a lion.

Shiki revolutionized the art of haiku writing, and

even coined the word *haiku*. He is acknowledged today, worldwide, as an artist who had wondrous vision; but I know of no record that states whether he ever saw the three things he truly wished to see.

26

LOOKING FOR A SIGN

THESE DAYS, Shiki would have no difficulty in locating a movie theater or bike race; but a wild lion would still be an impossibility in Japan.

For me, things are different. Any day could bring a chance sighting. Whenever I go out walking, I am aware of this possibility. I venture off trail as much as possible, zigzagging along the high ridges, investigating drainages, poking at rotten logs and leaf litter, looking for telltale signs. I try to find leaves or pebbles freshly turned, and wander the creek beds looking for muddy tracks. When walking the winding trails and fire roads, I travel the inside corners, taking the shortcuts a cougar itself would ordinarily take. And I stop, occasionally, to look at what might be behind me.

27

HARLEY

IF YOU SHOOT an arrow first, and then draw the target around it, you will always appear to have hit the bull's-eye. But I seemed to be standing like a lone arrow stuck in open ground, ringed not by the target but by circles of questions I couldn't answer. I had experienced some wonderful moments on the trail, but no matter how I looked at it, I had still not found a mountain lion. I had found scat and a few tracks, but not the living animal. Feeling a bit stymied, I wrote a letter to a person I'd never met. I felt certain that he could answer at least a few of my questions.

Harley Shaw lives in rural Arizona. From 1963 to 1990 he worked as a tracker and research biologist for the Arizona Game and Fish Department. He has also written two books on cougars, *A Mountain Lion Field Guide* and *Soul among Lions: The Cougar as Peaceful Adversary*. Harley is considered one of the world's great experts on finding mountain lions.

I wrote, telling him of the dilemma I was in, trying to explain a search I didn't fully understand myself, and asking in as subtle a way as possible for assistance, inspiration, and strong moral direction. I am surprised to this day that he bothered to answer. In a lengthy, handwritten, and densely worded letter, he essentially told me to give it up.

After detailing the unnecessary, futile, and highly superfluous nature of my venture, he wrote at the bottom of the second page, "I'll assume you will ignore all this advice." And then, warmly and tactfully, he advised me on several ways it might be most beneficial to proceed.

Later, I would reread this letter often, always beginning on page 3.

MELVILLE

ONCE AGAIN, I stood in front of the special place I sometimes visited. The old female cougar had been replaced by a large handwritten cardboard sign informing visitors that she had died. She had, years earlier, given birth to a number of young, the sign said, and had enjoyed a good life. The odd presumption and shallowness of this statement struck me as appalling.

True, she had performed well her ritual dance. She had gone without complaint through the motions of "enjoying her life." In reality, there was no life to be had in her situation. She had eaten the food given her, had borne her cubs, and then had paced her life away. One wonders how many miles she might have traveled in her imagination.

I took out my pen and notebook and sat beneath a tree, not knowing what I wanted to write. I saw the list of twenty random words that I had written here months earlier, and a quote from Melville where he refers to the "panther heart" of the sea.

I wondered if Melville had "enjoyed" his life. He had written one of the world's greatest books about searching; he had written one hundred and thirty-five chapters about a man going looking for a whale; and he had said, "There are some enterprises in which a careful disorderliness is the true method."

This was of course heartening to me. It would have been vivifying to anyone who was not exactly sure of what he was doing. Melville's Ahab had raged through *Moby Dick* with a single-minded purpose.

He had gone looking, not for a mere animal, but for revenge. Ahab had lost himself in questing. He had died in an act of discovery, but still not knowing what he'd found.

The phrase "panther heart" seemed to rise above the page. There was now one less cougar heart living and beating in this world, one less lion to be seen. I certainly did hope that she had enjoyed her life, or at least her existence. I walked back to where she'd been kept, and stared down into what appeared to be an ocean of emptiness. The packed-earth floor of her enclosure seemed to withhold some vital news, some secret that had slowly been pounded into it by a series of countless steps. This riddle had nothing to do with order or disorder, nothing to do with land or sea.

29

SEA TRIP

A FEW DAYS later, as if to assuage the grim visage of Ahab, I headed out to sea myself. A group of naturalists had organized a one-day whale-watching and birding trip, and I decided to go along. I figured a rest from mountain lion chasing might do me good.

We left the harbor in darkness, under clear skies, with the moon's reflection bouncing ahead of us in the water. At the first faint sign of sunrise, some of those on board began looking through binoculars, sweeping the almost invisible horizon and tracking impossibly dark birds against the nearly black sky. After a very few minutes, everything began to lighten as the sun rose slowly from behind the coastal foothills. We stood fastened to the rails, getting used to the feel of being on the ocean, practicing the art of staying upright while looking through high-powered glasses at specks far beyond our ordinary sight.

People began calling out the names of seabirds, slowly and occasionally at first, then more often and excitedly as the sunlight came up to its full force; Cassin's auklet, black scoter, glaucous-winged gull. Almost immediately, we were joined by a pod of Dall's porpoises, black-and-white streaks shooting back and forth under and along our bow, quick and powerful and almost never rising above the surface of the water. They charged ahead of us and then peeled off, not to be seen again.

A few miles offshore, things truly began to come alive. We began to find the jaeger, the skua, and the Sabine's gull. Thirty Pacific white-sided dolphins came hurtling past us, cutting through the wake of the boat, racing and bow-riding in front of us, leaping clear of the water and cartwheeling end-over-end before landing with a splash and then continuing on. They stayed with us for some time before they, also, disappeared. We began to see humpbacked whales, blue whales, and the black-footed albatross. This albatross, with a wingspan of seven feet, is still considered "small" by world standards, but it is the one most commonly seen in these waters. Extremely rare birds such as the light-mantled sooty albatross, the shy albatross, and the wandering albatross have also been sighted near here. The wandering albatross has a wingspan of up to twelve feet and is native to the Southern Hemisphere. Its neighbor, the South Polar skua, is born in Antarctica and nourished on parent-proffered penguin meat until it is mature enough to fly. Now in full daylight, we saw a few of these skuas passing overhead.

Our plan was to make a lazy one-hundred-mile loop out of the harbor, and to keep our eyes open for whatever we might see. When we'd lost all sight of land, we stopped to lay out an organic oil slick. Unrefined cod-liver oil was supplemented with plain popcorn and fish-bait scraps and soon had us surrounded by birds. The gulls, fulmars, and albatrosses wheeled overhead and then alighted and sat next to us on the water. They seemed unbothered as we scrambled for our bird books and cameras. For forty minutes or so we all sat there together on the open sea, birds and humans looking each other in the eye, rocking in the gentle swell. Then the boat hauled herself around and headed southward.

In the afternoon the wind came up, and the decks were periodically washed with seawater. We saw a few more whales—one of them a humpback with its flukes scarred by the raking of a killer whale's teeth—and then began the long trip back to land. The boat's passengers settled into corners, out of the way of the wind, and a few fell asleep. As we neared shore, word went out that we were among a phenomenally large population of *Aurelia aurita,* moon jellyfish. The trip leaders on board said they'd never seen so many. We jumped to the rails and saw millions of these animals, literally acres of them, surrounding us. They were so densely packed that the boat appeared to be moving through *Aurelia* rather than water. Staring down at them produced a nearly mesmeric effect. They opened and closed and swirled with the motion of the sea. One wondered how such great numbers of them were possible, how such a multitude of *anything* was possible.

And then we were out of them and into clear waters once again. By the time we'd traveled down the coast and reached the small harbor, the sun had set and darkness had descended.

After arriving home, as I sat at the kitchen table after spending thirteen hours at sea, I wondered what I'd done to myself. The whole house opened and closed and swirled like the *Aurelia*. It was a dizzying lesson in changing from one environment to another. Again, I asked myself what I was doing looking for cougars. I had, after all, just seen some very special and rare sights. What need was there, really, for me to continue looking for a mountain lion?

The boat trip had offered a refreshing change. There were no trees or rocks or hills for things to hide behind, just "above the surface" and "below the surface." This appeared to me so much like a Zen Buddhist insight that I nearly felt overcome with sudden wisdom. Then I realized that any so-called wisdom I was experiencing was merely another form of fatigue and dizziness; and as the room began swinging from side to side again, I stored away my sea gear and headed off for bed.

30

THE FOLLOWING MORNING

MELVILLE HAD written, "Meditation and water are wedded for ever." I thought of this the next morning as I poured a swirl of coffee into a still-unsteady cup. My physical body was mostly made of water, and today it was still being influenced by the sea. Though not a day old, the events of yesterday seemed like a meditative dream.

Zen teachers often tell students that this is the way it will be; things will continually arise and disappear; life is "a bubble, a phantasm, a flash of lightning"; form and substance are like "dew on the grass."

Yesterday, there had been seabirds flying into my life and out again. There had been dolphins, and a curved horizon. Today, that was all like a different life that had happened to someone else. After experiencing the ocean's great expanse, our kitchen felt like a small enclosure. I could almost feel myself beginning to pace. I could see the tracks of a cougar, overlaid by my own footprints, like dance steps someone had painted across the kitchen floor.

31

IKKYU AND WALKING MEDITATION

THE FIFTEENTH-CENTURY Zen master Ikkyu wrote, "For woodcutters and fishermen, knowledge and action are the same. Why would they need the carved furniture or the smooth wooden floors of Zen? With straw sandals and a walking stick, they travel through three thousand different worlds, sleeping on water, eating the wind."

The peripatetic nature of the outdoor traveler has been distilled into the Zen practice known as *kinhin*, or walking meditation. This formal, ritualized way of

walking is an extension of *zazen,* the seated meditation for which Zen is best known. It is still practiced
daily in Zen temples today.

When I scramble up the local mountain peaks, I'm
sometimes conscious of the lessons taught in the
meditation hall. There is an important relationship
between our breathing and the steps we choose to
take. Before tackling the steeper, higher elevations of
the Himalayas, trekkers are taught a technique
known as "the meditation step." They are instructed
to take one full breath between each step of the
climb they undertake. Over time, breathing and carrying one's self forward are joined together; one's
actions are forged within the body, without thought.
It takes practice to approach a summit in a slow and
measured way.

32

MORE DREAMS

OUR CONSCIOUSNESS and our subconscious
vision can also become interwoven in this way.

It was shortly after my day at sea that the mountain lion dreams began. One might think that after
all my searching and study, this would have happened much earlier. The first dream was as fleeting
and as realistic as any dream I've ever had: I was
driving out the Lucas Valley Road, in daylight, when
an animal raced through an adjacent open field,
crossed the road, and stopped dead in its tracks. It
was waiting for me. Its action was vivid and instan-
taneous. I was at first in doubt as to what the animal

was, and then recalled the three-foot-long tail that had streamed behind it as it ran. I was then certain that it was a cougar, and I was extremely elated as I stared at the exact spot where it awaited me.

When I awoke, the dream remained as clear and detailed as any scene in real life. I had gone from uncertainty to complete assurance, and now awakened, from exultation to a feeling of sudden loss. The entire experience—the abrupt, extreme ride of my emotions—lasted but a few seconds.

Since then, I have continued to experience periodic, anfractuous dreams similar to this one. They spread themselves out a few weeks apart. Each lasts for only a few moments; but they are all intense enough to awaken me. A salient feature of these dreams is their utter casualness. A lion crosses a path, drinks water from a stream, or sits in sunlight. There is never any foreboding of drama, confrontation, or danger. There is no hint of any significance or symbolic importance. Indeed, these many lion sightings, which occur only while I dream, have almost become nonevents. Yet they always seem to follow the same pattern; transporting me from doubt to absolute certainty, and then from short-lived jubilance to a regnant sense of loss.

33

CHIURA OBATA

"THE ART OF LIVING," Marcus Aurelius once said, "is more like wrestling than dancing."

Disquieted by my inability to find the thing I was

looking for and perplexed by my dreams, I did what a cougar itself would do; I began to gradually expand my territory. I tried to walk in a different direction and take an interest in other things.

One Saturday morning, my wife and I drove to San Francisco to see an exhibition of artwork by Chiura Obata. Obata was a painter and printmaker who had been born in Japan in 1885, and who had lived in northern California for many years. He had painted mountains of the Bay Area and the Sierra Nevada. He had been a professor of art at the University of California at Berkeley.

In the museum gallery, my wife and I went our separate ways. She was interested in a display case that contained an assortment of brushes, inks, and pigments that Obata used in creating his images. I was in another room, frozen in place, reading the printed card that referred to one of his paintings:

I had a strong determination to see the Tuolumne River, particularly the Water Wheel Falls so I started from Glen Aulin. The river bottoms are just big boulders so the water was very clear and I spotted many nice-sized trout but my mission was to sketch the Water Wheel Falls so I kept moving on the trail. A little rain began to fall and on the narrow trail I came upon a large deer lying on the ground. At first I thought it was shot by a hunter, I bent down to touch the deer which was still warm, then I noticed a mountain lion had chewed the animal's throat. I was a bit scared but I continued on the trail and soon as I approached I heard a sound like many fighter airplanes mingling in the sky and I reached the falls. The scenery was so different with rock formations like elephants next to diamond-shaped stones.

Obata sometimes painted very quickly, in the *sumi* style. Years of practicing these techniques enabled him to immediately capture, in black ink and colored water, exactly the picture he wished to portray. This rapid style of working, with no time spent on corrections or alterations, was exactly the right medium for capturing the quick and tumultuous flow of the river. The painting produced on this occasion, *Sounding River, Tuolumne Canyon* (1937), was painted even more quickly than was usual. The artist was well aware that a wild mountain lion was in the vicinity.

I regarded this river painting as I imagined Obata himself might have looked at it at river's edge. Standing there, fully enveloped in the overwhelming sound of roaring water, one would never be able to hear a mountain lion's approach. These fierce and delicate swirls of ink could be, as well as anything else, the very last things an artist might ever see of this world.

For me, at least for now, mountain lions seemed to constitute an inescapable condition. I encountered them everywhere I went. Even as I sought to distance myself from the search, Obata's mountain lion had sprung on me and caught me unaware. Seeing this painting of clamorous water brought to mind a Zen koan, and reminded me of the ancient riddle of the Sphinx. I couldn't recall what the riddle itself had been, but I knew for certain that the Sphinx had been half lion.

34

LOOKING AT ART

SOMETIMES, WHEN I stand before a work of art, I will close my eyes and then reopen them. The image before me becomes reborn with fresh appearance and renewed color, and I often see the painting or drawing in a different way.

When we close our eyes, we don't stop *seeing;* we start seeing darkness. We may, in fact, learn to see darkness quite well. We may even begin to prefer it.

I knew that, were I ever to encounter a wild mountain lion, I wouldn't have the luxury of looking at it like a work of art. A fleeting glimpse of it would, most likely, be all I'd be afforded. So many of life's great experiences seem to be garnered in this way; a long and arduous preparation followed by a rare performance or special occurrence. Many professional athletes and musicians dedicate great portions of their lives to living in this manner. The rest of us also spend a great part of our lives led by anticipation; working our way toward some brief satisfaction or objective, some relevant insight or split-second event that we hope will change our lives.

As I began to ponder darkness and the great many ways we look at things, an old Zen adage suddenly began to take on new relevance for me. It was the great master Seigen Ishin who said, "Before a person studies Zen, all mountains appear to be mountains, and rivers appear to be rivers. While studying Zen, these same mountains no longer seem to be mountains, and the rivers do not seem like rivers. But, after a person has completed their Zen study and attained a state of essential rest, the mountains once again appear to be mountains, and rivers are rivers just as before."

I had reached a stage in my cougar research when mountain lions no longer seemed to be mountain lions. They had never actually been visible to me, but now they seemed even farther away. The very thought of them began to drag me into the shadows.

My Zen teachers had cautioned me to be prepared for anything, but never to "expect" or "anticipate" or "rely upon" anything. In my zeal for finding *kimmo no shishi*, the golden-haired lion, I seemed to have gradually forgotten much of this advice. Although I'd had new and unforgettable experiences, I now found myself faced with a declining resolve and an increasing doubt. Looking for a mountain lion was beginning to take on the qualities of a wayward stroll up a blind alley on a moonless night.

Perhaps my idea of finding a cougar was terribly misguided. Perhaps there *were* no mountain lions after all.

PART TWO

MOUNTAINS ARE
NOT
WHAT THEY SEEM

MCKINLEY

I AWOKE ONE morning to discover that, sometime during the previous night, our cat McKinley
had gone blind. She stood with a bloody nose in the
middle of our living room. I cleaned her face and
could clearly tell that she was unable to see anything. I had no idea what had caused her to lose her
sight, but surmised that it might have been a stroke
of some kind. Afterward, she had either fallen from
the couch or walked into something solid and blood-
ied her nose. She had grown quite old, and now her
life had suddenly become more precarious.

We confined her to a small area where she could
find her food, water, and litter box by scent and feel.
I remember watching her for long periods as she sat,
unseeing, in any warm and random patch of available sunlight.

In another week, without any sense of day or
night, her actions quieted and she lost her will to go
on. The world as she knew it had disappeared, and
shortly thereafter, she herself was gone.

36

BORGES

AS I WATCHED McKinley resting quietly in the
sunshine, a subtle question began to occur to me:

What is the difference between being blind and looking for something one might never see?

I had, in the course of my research on mountain lions, run across the writings of Jorge Luis Borges concerned with tigers, panthers, and his own blindness. The many afternoons he spent staring, without seeing, into the cages of the great cats at the Buenos Aires zoo seemed uncomfortably close to some of my own recent experiences.

Borges had often chosen tigers as his theme in poetry and in prose. He wrote of tigers appearing in his dreams and of tigers in reality. He spoke of the utter incompetence of his trying to conjure these animals while sleeping; of the awkward and enfeebled shapes they seemed to take, of the imperfections of their form and size, and of their fleeting existence. He also wrote of once meeting a genuine tiger, face-to-face, through the generosity of a friend of his who worked for Animal World, an exotic park without cages or steel bars. This tiger had put his forepaws on Borges's head and licked his face. Borges had experienced what he termed a "terrified happiness," and later wrote that this animal had real smell and weight but, in actuality, seemed no more real to him than the dreamed tigers or those he'd read about in books.

Borges's blindness began to intrigue me. And I recalled the article I had read so long ago about the speed of light and the tau neutrino. I remembered the many admonitions I'd heard as a Zen student to open up my eyes and stop wandering blindly through my own treasured life. What did it mean to open up my eyes? What did it mean to really see?

JUNEAU AND EXISTENCE

THE ZEN MASTER Dogen once said, "The moon does not necessarily appear at night; and nighttime is not necessarily dark. When thinking about these things, we should be open and not limit ourselves to the narrow views held by human beings."

I had tried to share some of McKinley's blindness with her, just as Borges had shared his blindness with the pumas, panthers, and tigers on display at the Buenos Aires zoo. I began to reflect upon various types and qualities of vision; and it was then that I recalled an incident that I had read about many years before in a book about Alaska.

A young man living just outside the Juneau city limits had been blinded by one swipe of the forepaw of a wild bear. The man had recovered from the attack but was badly scarred and left without eyesight or any sense of smell or taste. He had moved to Seattle to live out the rest of his life. He could never live in Alaska again, he said—not because he was afraid, but because it was too beautiful. He didn't mind being blind so much in a big city where all he was missing was the sunlight glaring from glassed-in office buildings and overcrowded freeways; but being blind in Alaska, while surrounded by incredible beauty, was a challenge he could not withstand.

There have always been those who insist that we are forever surrounded by beauty, but that many of us have difficulty in perceiving it. Navajo spiritual leaders encourage their followers to walk in beauty. But Zen teachers ask their students what beauty is and how they can ever hope to find it.

I was once having a casual conversation with a friend of mine who is a Zen teacher. He asked me what I'd been doing lately. I said that I'd been studying mountain lions and had been spending a great deal of time roaming the country, looking for them. It was then that he dropped a small Zen bomb. "Do they exist?" he asked. My friend had once again resumed his role as teacher. He was not questioning whether or not there were lions in this part of the world. He was asking me to respond to the very nature of existence.

38

THE HEART SUTRA

MCKINLEY WAS NOT just our house cat. She was a uniquely arranged concentration of billions upon billions of atoms. (The number of atoms estimated to form a cat is believed to be around 10 to the 27th power.) McKinley was totally unaware that she was a mass of atoms. She did not know that she was "a gray domestic short hair."

Everything we find in our universe can be described. Whether or not this depiction is successful (or accurate) can be a highly debatable and subjective matter. Each of us has our own way of seeing things and of telling others about what we see.

As a Zen student, I was often cautioned against confusing any description of the world with the

world itself. I was informed that to verbally delin-
eate the characteristics of an object is merely to create a chain of descriptive words, and that words are
often the weakest method of portraying any reality.

To further illustrate this point, I was given a copy
of the Heart Sutra, a one-page reduction of Buddhist
thought said to contain the essence of Mahayana
teachings. The purpose of this single page of text is
to help Zen students articulate the most important
questions confronting them, the ones that lead many
of them to study Zen in the first place: What are we?
What is reality? What is the meaning of existence?

Scientists have also asked themselves these same
questions. Through direct, methodical study, they
have attempted to define these same uncertainties
and to discover some reasonable responses to them.

More and more, it appears that Zen masters and
scientists have much in common. Aside from their
unending questioning, there appears to be much
agreement on how they view phenomenal existence,
on how they see this "world of emptiness" filled
with all manner of limitlessly compelling forms.

39

BLUE CLIFF RECORD

A CLASSIC COLLECTION of Zen writings
known as the Hekiganroku, or "Blue Cliff Record,"
deals with both the way we see things and the way
the universe is put together. In one section, a monk
asks his teacher, "When I do not see, why do you not
see my not-seeing?" The Zen master answers that

seeing itself is not something that can be seen; that seeing is not a thing we can show to someone else; and that even when we cannot see, the golden-haired lion (our own buddha nature) always stands with eyes wide open and ears erect.

This ancient text goes on to quote another Zen master, Engo, who speaks of "blinding cataracts in the eyes" and "groping one's way blindly along a barricade." He then tells us that every single atom in the universe can only take us partway toward finding what it is we're really looking for; that if we were able to unravel the mystery surrounding every single atomic particle in the cosmos, we'd still be only halfway there.

40

SMALL MIRACLES

MY MOUNTAIN LION studies eventually led me to investigate the lion's vision and perception, and how these qualities might compare with our own.

The cougar might be described as an extremely effective and biologically successful machine. When it hunts for food, all parts of the animal work together as a unit. No dividing line separates its physical or mental processes from the activity in which it is engaged. And there is no greater element on which it depends for survival than its highly evolved ability to see.

Cats are justly renowned for their eyesight, in both darkness and the light of day. A cat's eyes are small miracles of design, miracles that allow the outside world to come in. Both the lens and cornea are sharply curved, creating a large anterior chamber and, in effect, bringing the retina closer to the lens. Cats have extremely sensitive retinas, the dense layers of light-receptor cells forming the back of each eyeball. Behind the retina, there is another reflective layer called the *tapetum lucidum* (Latin for "bright carpet"), which bounces light back out through the retina again, giving it twice its ability to function. The tapetum may have as many as fifteen layers of cells. When, in darkness, we chance to shine a light on a nocturnal animal such as a cat, the resultant reflection (eye-shine) is light which has been doubly processed and returned again by this shining carpet.

In order not to be put at a disadvantage in brightly lit conditions, many cats also have a twofold way of closing down their pupils (the dark centers of their eyeballs). A cat's pupils are able to expand and contract, much as our own, depending on whether the light is harsh or largely unavailable. However, the domestic cat, and other felines, also has a specific muscular structure surrounding their eyes, the ciliary muscles, that enables them to draw their pupils into thin slits, allowing them to better control their vision under a wide variety of circumstances and conditions. They command light as few other animals can.

Distance information for cats, like that in almost all predators, is the result of highly developed binocular vision—both eyes facing forward and able to focus on a single point—and having a compatible brain complexity. Cats have greater binocular vision than that of any other carnivore.

A mountain lion's eyes are proportionately large when compared to those of other animals, and their pupils are correspondingly large as well. A cougar's pupils, unlike the house cat's, are forever round and are designed to stay that way. They have a 75-degree greater field of vision than that of a human being, and their pupils open to a size three times as large as ours. The retinas of cats and humans alike contain both rods and cones. Cones are gathered near the center of the retina in both species, but a cat's retinas contain a much greater concentration of rods than cones, and this is what gives them their excellent ability to see in darkness. Our own retinas possess more cones, giving us greater visual acuity and more discernment in judging colors and shadings but failing us mightily when we are lost in the dark. A cougar's color sense has not been adequately studied, but house cats can distinguish several basic colors.

When a cat shows aggression, its mouth is nearly closed, its ears are erect, and the pupils of its eyes are small and narrowed. In a defensive posture, a cat's teeth are exposed, its ears are flattened against the head, and its pupils are opened wide.

This is the point at which the observer would do well to stand back and advance no farther. All cats, domestic or wild, possess an almost uncanny sensitivity to objects moving within their line of sight. Movement often triggers a cat's "attack response," which is why deer and other prey "freeze" instinctively once a predator is detected.

In this situation, a prey animal is caught in the open on its own bright carpet. It is wildly exposed and vulnerable. Capture is often inevitable.

THE CHINESE SAGES

THE ANCIENT CHINESE sages seemed to know a thing or two about darkness.

Lao-tsu said:

Mysteries and revelations both come from the same place. The gate leading to all understanding is darkness beyond darkness. Colors only make us blind. When we look for truth, we don't see it and describe it as nonexistent or indistinct. Real clarity of vision is seeing what can't be seen.

Te-ching said:

When our eyes travel freely throughout the world of form, they can no longer discern what is real.

Ho-shang Kung said:

Searching gets us nowhere. The answer is found in darkness, in stillness, and in our own wild nature.

FOREBODING

I HAD COME to a kind of impasse as far as finding a mountain lion. Perhaps the remedy for this shaken resolve, this overshadowing of my own instinctive curiosity, did wait for me somewhere in darkness.

All of my searching had been done in daylight, even though I knew the cats were more likely to be out at night. I began recalling the many trails I'd traveled in search of tracks or other indications that a mountain lion had passed by, and I tried to envision what these same trails would be like in darkness. I'd taken a few nocturnal rambles in years past, looking for owls or studying stars, and I could summon in my imagination a vision of moonlit fire roads and of being stranded on the sides of hills on moonless nights. I could even feel the chill of the night air and the coldness of boots soaked by wet grass or unseen rivulets of water.

I'd never really thought of walking through cougar country alone in the dead of night. I wondered about my own judgment even in considering such an action. The thought of making a regular practice of walking in such a deliberately blind and disadvantageous way brought an immediate and ominous foreboding.

And yet there were good reasons to consider doing such a thing. I would be active when the cats were most active; I could use the flashlight to better control illumination when examining tracks; I would be approaching almost everything in a radically different frame of mind; and lastly, and perhaps most importantly, I hadn't had any luck in discovering a lion in daylight.

43

DARKNESS AT DEVIL'S GULCH

THE TRAIL AT Devil's Gulch was by no one's standard a difficult trail to follow or to walk upon. It was much more a road than a trail, and it meandered for most of its length along an easy, quiet creek. There were no obstructions one needed to confront, no precipices one might inadvertently step from. The ground was level for long stretches, and any hills a hiker might encounter were gradual and inviting. This winding path seemed a good place to choose for my first walk at night.

My inclination has always been to rise early, rather than stay up late. So, after a fitful sleep, I put a small flashlight, a wool cap, and a bag of peanuts into my jacket pockets and drove in darkness to the parking area across the road from Devil's Gulch Trail. At three o'clock in the morning, on a midweek day, I still felt fortunate to encounter no other cars on my way there.

The night air was bracing, and I felt greatly alive. Only a thin parenthesis of moonlight hid somewhere up behind the trees. I crossed the main road and began walking up the paved-over section of the trail. The night wasn't completely dark, but it was dark enough to appear somewhat threatening. Although I chose my steps with care, I felt much more awkward than was usual. There had been dozens of cougar sightings in this area throughout the years, and I was acutely aware of the inappropriateness of my being here at this hour. To say that I felt vulnerable would be a bit of an understatement. I felt deerlike.

After cutting silently and cautiously through the darkness for a few minutes, I left the pavement behind and stepped onto the dirt-and-gravel section of the main trail. I could distinguish a subtle change in darkness between the surrounding hills and the sky overhead. The crunch of rocks and pebbles beneath my boot soles seemed amplified beyond reason. I was certain my steps could be heard from miles away.

Suddenly, I nearly leapt straight from the ground as a violent, startling explosion of sound and activity erupted just a few feet from me. My heart pounded unmercifully as I realized there was a man standing there in the darkness. My eyes must have been opened to their maximum extreme. They seemed to inhale moonlight the way a suffocating person might suck in air. I could see the man beginning to crouch, trying to get a better look at me; and I could see something long and sharp in his hand.

At that moment, I possessed nothing close to reason, but I acted out of pure instinct. I made my voice as low and calm as possible, and said, "I'm not going to hurt you. I'm only out here for a walk." The man said something indiscernible and then backed away from the trail.

I had almost stumbled upon this lone, homeless man. He'd been sleeping here, well off the main road, beneath a jet-black plastic tarpaulin, and he'd clearly been terrified by my approach. I stood for a moment, staring intently in the direction in which he'd headed. Then I turned about and headed back toward where I'd begun my walk. I removed the flashlight from my jacket pocket and pivoted its small but reassuring beam of light from one side of the trail to the other, all the way back to where my truck was parked.

My dark explorations had, on this occasion, not taken me very far. I was effectively defeated before I'd even begun.

44

NIGHT WALKING

ISAAC NEWTON once said, "Never did I get bigger headaches then when I was working on the problem of the moon."

And Henry Thoreau, after writing his masterpiece, *Walden*, intended that his next labor would be to write a book about the moon. He traveled Massachusetts extensively, giving lectures about the moon and keeping elaborate notes on the subject. It is said that, when walking at night, Thoreau couldn't bear to hear the sounds of his own footsteps on gravel, and would always walk the grassy edges of the roads and paths.

I knew the grating sound of my own footsteps quite well; but gradually the relationship between these sounds and the impenetrable night and my desire to go walking through it coalesced and became more reconciled. Although I never felt truly at ease in the dark, or dared to be unwary, I seemed to grow more accustomed to walking underneath the grand dome of an unlit sky. I became more familiar with the effects of night vision and a dimmed color sense.

During off hours, I reread Homer's classic descriptions of the Cimmerians, a people who inhabited a land of perpetual darkness. (Homer himself had been blind.) And I reread the poetry of John Milton (totally blind) and the prose of James Joyce (partially blind) and Borges (sightless, but for my purposes perhaps the most insightful of all).

I soon found myself deep in a circadian rhythm of nighttime exploration. When I hiked the hills at night, I grew more comfortable with the enigmatic and the stubbornly unseeable. I was glad to get away from the perpetual busyness of daytime. (Milton had in fact coined the descriptive word *pandemonium*.) I began to search for night-blooming flowers and nocturnal insects. I relished the sight of constellations, streaking meteors, long-range aircraft, and man-made satellites. I listened for skittering animals and for the wind; for the urgent hooting of owls and the sounds of nearby running water.

All of this overriding silence and darkness reminded me of time spent in the Zen meditation halls; the quiet rustling of clothing, the growling stomachs, the throat-clearing, the sniffling, the swallowing. I was now made alert to my own sounds while unscrewing the lid from the thermos, rummaging through the pack, scratching the pen across rough paper while attempting to take notes.

Even the unilluminated darkness seemed refreshing when compared with staring at so many blank Zen-washed walls.

I found further comfort in the slightly ambiguous aromas that traveled upon the nighttime air: the faint smells of bay leaves, moist earth, horse manure, salt water, wood smoke, or relic whiffs of skunk.

However, throughout all of this deeply sensory experience, I never forgot why I was out walking at night. There was nothing I listened for with more intensity than for the absolute silence of an approaching mountain lion. With my embarrassingly poor olfactory senses, I still troubled every breeze. And at least once a minute, I flashed a strong beam of light outward and around me in a complete circle, looking for the greenish gold shine of any double-reflecting eyes that might be looking back at me.

At such times I felt like a displaced lighthouse keeper who had wandered far from shore. I would then turn off the light and walk in darkness, sometimes reaching out for a handrail I knew was never there.

45

INVENTORY

THE COMMON REFLECTORS made from glass or plastic, used as safety devices on automobiles and along roadways, were originally called "cat's-eyes." Like the *tapetum lucidum,* their job is to reflect light directly back in the direction from which it originates.

Directed light can also be used in another way. While hiking during the daytime, I had twice come upon hidden remote cameras set up by the National Park Service. These weatherproof cameras were placed at strategic sites within the more remote areas of the Point Reyes National Seashore, along game trails and quiet creeks. They were installed and maintained by two Park Service research biologists, Gary Fellers and David Pratt. The unattended cameras were triggered by a special sensor, a pencil-thin beam of light that, when broken by the movement of an unsuspecting animal, would trip a floodlight and camera rigged to a nearby tree and cause the animal to take its own photograph.

The quality of these photographs varied greatly. Each camera lens had only one fixed focus. And local weather conditions created clear nights as well as those enshrouded in coastal fog. The park covers approximately seventy thousand acres, and the cameras were used there over a two-year period. A total of 4,692 exposures were developed, and the animals photographed were as follows: 968 mule deer, 800 gray foxes, 729 raccoons, 674 brush rabbits, 384 fallow deer, 381 striped skunks, 357 bobcats, 140 human beings, 76 opossums, 59 dogs, 29 badgers, 27 gray squirrels, 7 mountain lions, 6 domestic cats, 6 coyotes, 3 tule elk, 3 black-tailed jackrabbits, 1 red fox, and 1 spotted skunk.

Birds were captured on film as well. Among these were 9 burrowing owls, 5 short-eared owls, 5 turkey vultures, 4 American robins, 3 scrub jays, 2 varied thrushes, 2 Say's phoebes, 2 northern harriers, 2 common ravens, 1 white-crowned sparrow, 1 western bluebird, 1 Stellar's jay, 1 red-tailed hawk, 1 red-shouldered hawk, 1 black phoebe, and a California quail.

One must remember that these numbers relate to photographs taken, not to the actual number of animals present in the environment. Several of these creatures undoubtedly took their own portrait more than once.

On at least one other occasion, another remote, hidden camera was used in this area. The nature photographer Michael Sewell, while collaborating with his friend and fellow photographer Galen Rowell on their book *Bay Area Wild*, tried this method as well. For a period of four years, Sewell stationed remote, motion-activated cameras on Mount Tamalpais and Mount Diablo, trying to obtain a photograph of a mountain lion. Although fresh tracks were sometimes found near the cameras, the cougars themselves failed to break the beam of light, and their photographs were never taken.

46

THE CONSTANT SECRET

MOUNTAIN LIONS have one constant secret; the immediate awareness of where they are. Their solitary wanderings preclude the modern human obsession with cell phones, pagers, e-mail, the Internet, and such. The lions prefer being alone and undiscovered. They need no Global Positioning System, no post office box or area code, to tell them where they are. Their world is without artificial designations or unnecessary connections. They move as naturally as a flame, full of life's energy and totally self-contained.

47

PLAYING THE ODDS

STEPPING LIKE a thief, I have been following a broken path through a sprawl of blackberry vines. The wisdom of rambling through the shrubbery of Mountainlionland in the dark and near-dark of night could certainly be called into question by anyone with even a rudimentary knowledge of predatory behavior in animals. Still, statistically speaking, this sort of exploration is much safer than taking a comparable walk through the nearest urban neighborhood at a similar hour.

I am in greater danger while driving my truck to the trailhead than I will ever be in while walking in the dark. There is a greater risk of my being hit by a falling tree than of my being attacked by a cougar. The odds were something I sometimes thought about on the long drives home.

Being out on the trail at night seemed to bring me in closer contact with my emotions. I was often lonely in a profound way, not for human companionship, but for something even deeper. I traveled through a landscape of obstacles, and at times felt totally disoriented, not knowing where to go next. Then I would experience a lilting sense of freedom, and I'd be completely at ease in a world without visible forms, boundaries, connections, rules, embarrassments, or any need of attainment. Like many other people, I felt rather insignificant when viewing the stars and planets overhead, but using charts and field guides enabled me to recognize and become familiar with even a few of these distant points of light.

Darkness became the great equalizer. In the deepening night, everything I'd ever seen or known seemed to be included in my thoughts at once. I sensed a heightened reason and alertness in my walking. There was a "wholeness" about being out at night that I hadn't perceived in daylight. Perhaps this was simply because I sensed fewer distractions, or because I was taking a different approach. For whatever reason, I was beginning to find these nighttime excursions enjoyable, and I began to relax and grow more confident each time out.

48

OLD NEWS AND NEW NEWS

IT HAD BEEN months since I'd watched anything on television. Once a week, I read through the *San Francisco Chronicle* or *New York Times* to learn what was going on in the rest of the world, but my definition of "news" had changed.

My big stories had become my own encounters: the rifle-crack sound of a breaking oak limb, a massive display of meteor showers, a singing in the middle of night that I couldn't identify.

I became my own weather report, because I was in it. I had learned to read the nuances of a changing front by feel. My predictions were not infallible, but they were immediate, and they were of consequence to no one else.

The sports scene, also, had become strictly personal. I was a one-man team, in much better shape than I was at the beginning of the season. I had a perfect record: no wins, no losses, no injuries.

It was difficult to understand, sometimes, why the entire countryside wasn't filled with people walking at night.

49

SOUND AND SILENCE

AFTER GOING on several local forays, I decided to revisit some of the outlying locations I'd covered earlier in my wanderings.

Now it was near nightfall, and I was sitting on a rock situated high up on the ridge that rises above the Green Gulch Farm Zen Center. Another boulder stood nearby. Its surface was glazed with moisture, and the way the remaining traces of light touched it made it appear to be covered in snow.

In the midst of the darkened Zen Center below, someone was setting out old-fashioned oil lamps along the walkways. Green Gulch residents had long followed a regimen of conservation. Along with strict management of water resources, extensive recycling programs, and other energy-saving procedures beneficial to the community, those who lived here were urged to follow two other "uncommon" environmental practices:

1. Conservation of Silence—Students are expected to make an effort to minimize talking,

and maintain silence from 7:30 P.M. through breakfast the next day. This reduces human impact on the soundscape of Green Gulch substantially, allowing the voices of birds, frogs, wind, and fog to be more present. During one-day and seven-day retreats, participants remain in silence the entire time, cultivating mindfulness of others living in the valley.

2. Conservation of Darkness—Light pollution is common in urban areas, severely reducing access to the night sky. Many schoolchildren in cities never see the moon or stars because of street, building, and highway lighting. At Green Gulch, night lighting is restricted to accommodate minimal safety needs. Otherwise, the hills remain dark and wild, an invitation to taste their original state of mind.

These recommendations are among those set forth in an eight-page document entitled *Environmental Practice at Green Gulch Zen Center,* written by Stephanie Kaza and distributed to all residents.

As I watched the lamps being set out below, I recalled the time, decades ago, when I was still attending high school in San Jose. Whenever I had difficulty grappling with teenage confusion and despair, I would drive up into the foothills of Mount Hamilton at night and look out over the lights of the great valley. After a time, my own tribulations would seem inconsequential. I would lose myself in following the lights of a single automobile traveling alone along a suburban street. My problems became secondary when I considered the magnitude of so many people's lives down in the valley below.

Tonight, I was sitting again on the high side of a mountain. Only five or six lanterns could be seen. The shining boulder near me had disappeared in the darkness, and the only thing interrupting the silence was the occasional plangent sound of an ocean wave breaking at Muir Beach.

Sounds have always been of special importance in Zen Buddhist teachings: the trickle of running water, the crisp clink of an errant pebble striking bamboo, the *mokugyo,* the *han,* the *unpan,* and all the other various bells, wooden clackers, and gongs in the temple.

The venerated Chinese teacher Lin-chi, who died in the year 866 and is known as Rinzai in Japan, once interrupted the silence with a shout that was said to have nearly cracked the universe. His students sometimes produced a weak emulation of this shout when asked to present evidence of their own understanding. Later on, this empty-headed mimicry grew so pervasive and distasteful that some Zen teachers actually fined their students for doing it. In this way, the universe was kept safe, and the students were asked to come up with something a little more original when trying to express themselves.

Breaking the silence can sometimes be a shortcut to cracking open the mysteries of the universe. But for now, I'm quite content to sit here quietly. There is only the infrequent shout of a distant ocean wave to rise above the regulated whisper of my own breathing. Soon, even these sounds fade.

THE HUNTER

IF SOMEONE WERE to see me sitting here on this rock in the dark, they would not know that I was hunting for a mountain lion. There is no reful-gent moon to light the sky. I have no night-vision tel-escopes or spy cameras. I have no pack of hunting dogs. Certainly, there are no weapons here. If I am hunting mountain lions, most folks would find me pathetically ill-prepared.

The Spanish philosopher José Ortega y Gasset once pointed out that philosophers from Plato to Aristotle often used words like *venator* and *thereutes* to describe what it was they did. These words meant "to go hunting."

Today's philosophers still search the world for answers to their questions. They "hunt" continuous-ly, night and day.

Sitting here in the almost total darkness, I won-der whether I'm a hunter or a philosopher, a track-er or a mere fool wasting my time. I remove the small flashlight from my pocket and break open the worn notebook. Attempting to assess my current situation, I write out six scrawled words: "ambigu-ous motives," "unfulfilled objectives," and "dubi-ous denouement."

IKKYU AND ORTEGA Y GASSET

THE VALUE OF any enterprise is in completely experiencing what happens. When the Zen master Ikkyu extolled the virtues of hunters, fishermen, and woodcutters, he did so because he saw the way in which they paid attention to things. They were always aware of the weather and the time of night or day. They paid particular attention to anything out of place in their environment: an unusual swirl of water, a distracting sound, a change in the color or texture of moss, moist earth, or scattered stones. They noticed the flight patterns of insects and the sudden rising of birds. They never, ever, took anything for granted, and everything they thought or did became an exercise in entering the unknown. When cutting down a tree or following a deer into a shaded thicket, they soon learned that the ground they stood upon could be a very unpredictable place.

Zen teachers found these activities to be splendid metaphors. They urged their students to behave in a like manner, and heralded the no-nonsense practicality of those who spent their lives in wild and natural surroundings. Teachers pointed out the benefits of observing wild animals themselves, emphasizing their alertness and acuity and praising their lack of pride and self-pity.

But it was Ortega y Gasset who declared that both meditation and hunting could leave a person feeling empty-handed. Both Socrates and Plato had hunted, in both senses of the word, and had often felt the sting of being on the losing end.

Whenever I found myself ruminating too much about what I was doing, or beginning to fret about what it was that compelled me to chase around at night, I would think of Ortega's words. I brightened at remembering a saying of his that I had read long ago: "The only rational response to an animal that's obsessed with eluding you is to pursue it." Recalling this quotation was almost enough to make me think I might be doing something rational after all.

52

NEW PREPARATIONS

EVEN AN IMPROPER boldness can sometimes have its place. The renegade Zen master Ikkyu broke Buddhist precepts and civil laws alike, yet he was one of the greatest figures in Zen's long history.

Once, while Ikkyu was still studying Zen with his teacher, Kaso, he decided he needed an afternoon away. He secured a small boat and rowed out onto Lake Biwa in order to meditate alone and undisturbed. As he drifted languidly across the waves, he fell asleep. He awoke suddenly to the sound of a crow calling from the shore far away and found himself fully enlightened. He rowed to shore quickly and hurried to confront his teacher. Ikkyu told Kaso everything that had happened to him and what he was experiencing at that moment. "What you describe to me is enlightenment," said Kaso, "but not the enlightenment of the Buddha ancestors, not the enlightenment of a real master." "Ha!" Ikkyu replied with audacity. "Who cares about Buddha and ancestors?

This kind of enlightenment is good enough for me!" Kaso's face broke into a wide grin. "THAT is the Zen of the Buddha ancestors. You are indeed a master!"

I WAS NOT EXACTLY floating on Lake Biwa. I felt more like a person up a creek. It was not that I was regretful of having spent so much time looking for something that didn't want to be found. I had learned a great deal and had begun experiencing life in a new way. However, the fact remained that I still had not seen a mountain lion. If darkness held the answer, perhaps I needed to engage it on a wider scale. I had walked through it, and sat meditating in it, and now it seemed the only thing left to do was to drive through it, and to keep driving until I discovered some form of light.

I would drive to where the lions were. There were plenty of two-lane roads in my part of the country that passed through prime cougar habitat but carried very little late-night traffic. I would prowl these roads, driving as slowly as was safe, with high-beamed lights raking the countryside. I would hope, at the very least, to see the shining eyes of the animal I had spent so much time seeking.

I prepared for my first low-speed mounted safari by stocking my Isuzu Trooper with a variety of creature comforts: a larger thermos bottle for coffee, a few tins of peppermint Altoids, an aluminum lunch box filled with foods that would never spoil, and several new tape cassettes. I didn't bother with any of the so-called spoken-word recordings, feeling that these might be too distracting. Instead, I leaned liberally in the direction of soothing instrumentals: assorted woodwind quintets and string trios, and the ballad collections of Bill Evans, John Coltrane, and Miles Davis. If I grew weary and needed to get pumped up, I could always switch over to the car's AM radio, where the airwaves were filled with rappers, Faith Hill, Travis Tritt, Smash Mouth, and Steely Dan.

I had a feeling that this just might work; that I just might catch a glimpse of a lion. In any event, I'd be much more comfortable than I had been while struggling blindly through underbrush or sitting on a sharp and unforgiving rock. I would be able to stop whenever I wanted to, and I could travel as far as I wished.

There were four routes nearby that I felt might be productive: the long road out to Pierce Point, the slightly longer road that came to an abrupt end near the Point Reyes Lighthouse, the road out to Limantour Beach, and the distant looping drive between Point Reyes Station and Nicasio, by way of the Nicasio Reservoir. There had been confirmed mountain lion sightings in all of these regions within the past few months, and none of the roads were much traveled upon late at night. All four of these routes had promise. They seemed four perfect places to test whether this new kind of undertaking would have any probative value.

53

TOMALES POINT

AS AN ASTUTE bumper sticker once suggested, not all of those who appear to be wandering are lost.

The valley where my wife and I live, the San Geronimo Valley, was long ago considered to be part of the Spanish empire, and later, part of Mexico. It was subsequently owned by, among other people, Joseph Warren Revere, the grandson of the American revolutionary hero Paul Revere. It has been home to world-famous musicians and movie stars, and it claims the largest remaining population of coho salmon in the state of California.

Tonight, within ten minute's drive of our house, two dozen deer have either frozen in place or fanned outward, away from my approaching headlights. It's easy to see why mountain lions favor this area. The deer are blacktails, a smaller coastal species closely related to mule deer (another black-tailed ungulate), and found from the Sierra Nevada to the Rockies. These native deer are ubiquitous; their only enemies are bobcats, cougars, coyotes, dogs, and inattentive drivers.

The deer are in turn a threat to almost anything growing in the ground. They eat garden plants, forbs, flowers, grass, and shrubbery. On one occasion they ate a small madrone tree standing near our house. They even ate part of our porch. Although they are usually strict herbivores, they have been known at times to sample spawned-out salmon.

After driving through the still-sleeping villages of Woodacre, San Geronimo, Forest Knolls, and Lagunitas, I enter the heavily forested area that surrounds Samuel P. Taylor State Park. This parkland includes Devil's Gulch, Mount Barnabe, and the site of the first paper mill on the Pacific Coast, the Pioneer Paper Mill, which supplied paper to the entire coast and furnished newsprint to the San Francisco newspapers of that time, the *Call*, the *Alta*, and the *Evening Bulletin*. In 1915 the last of the mill's buildings burned to the ground, but remains of their foundations can still be seen today.

On this night, however, I see nothing but dashboard lights and the road directly in front of me. As I pass the trailhead to Devil's Gulch, I wonder vaguely about the homeless man I startled on my nighttime walk there, and about the bobcat I'd seen there earlier, in the daylight.

It's certainly very different driving late at night. There are no large recreational vehicles weaving their way into my traffic lane or herds of synthetically attired bicyclists riding the center line. It all seems much more civilized here, in fact, with no other people around. I can feel my shoulders relax as I wind through the darkened forest.

Before long, I enter open rangeland and approach the environs of the Golden Gate National Recreation Area and the Point Reyes National Seashore. The road I travel (named for the explorer and privateer Sir Francis Drake) seems to end at its intersection with State Highway 1, in the small town of Olema. But later, Sir Francis Drake Boulevard (called a "highway" by state transportation optimists) will continue another twenty-three miles or so to the Point Reyes Lighthouse.

It was near Olema, years ago, that I saw my first Marin County coyotes. And it was here that a friend of mine, while drying his laundry at the Olema Campground, watched a mountain lion saunter past the laundry room as silently and slowly as a fading color.

From this point on, I will pay extra attention to anything I see by the roadside, any hint of uncommon movement, any sparkle of light. Chances are indeed slim that I will see a cougar, but I've been seeing deer all the way out here, and deer are what the cougar looks for.

Slowly, I turn onto the Bear Valley Road and drive past the turnoffs for the visitor's center and for Limantour Road. There are brush rabbits about, and a black-tailed hare. I see something else I'm not sure of, a raccoon or a gray fox, moving away too quickly to distinguish. Along the roadsides and among the shrubbery, isolated interruptions of broken taillight bits and shattered glass, like shining eyes, call for my immediate evaluation. Occasionally I see other things that appear to be mammalian but which turn out to be lost shoes or fallen branches. I'm still relaxed but much more alert, unwilling to concede anything to the darkness beyond the edges of the road.

I make the dogleg back onto Sir Francis Drake and drive slowly through the communities of Inverness Park and Inverness, both pleasantly situated on the western shores of Tomales Bay. Soon, just beyond Inverness, I reach Pierce Point Road, the long road heading northward through dairy lands and open country and ending at Tomales Point, also known as Pierce Point. Ahead are dark miles of double yellow lines, fence posts, and mileage markers. This area is the northern extreme of the peninsula and of the Point Reyes National Seashore. Tomales Point is home to a large and burgeoning population of tule elk, reintroduced here by the National Park Service in 1978–79 and doing quite well. Needless to say, wherever there are elk, there are also mountain lions.

Shortly after turning onto Pierce Point Road, I look up to see the silhouette of a great horned owl perched on a power line against a faint smear of moonlight. This long-ingrained symbol of Halloween quickly sets me to thinking of the Segaki ceremony at Green Gulch so long ago. I remember reciting the names of mountain lion fatalities, and I remember how I'd hoped to see a lion that day as I hiked the hills above. Now I'm here, in the middle of the night, driving my battered Trooper between hidden hillocks of cow manure and open pasture, all beneath an unending sky. I'm not sure many people would define this as progress.

Pierce Point Ranch is at the end of the road, at least of this particular road. A white wooden fence surrounds the visitors' center, and there are interpretive signs and a trail that heads north until there's no more land. Being out on the tip of the peninsula, at the end of this trail, is sometimes like being at sea.

Before I reach the road's end, I park on its grassy edge, shift into neutral, and pull on the hand brake. My headlights illuminate great racks of elk antlers forty yards in front of me. The rest of the animals are just below my line of sight, on a dark slope that leads down to the ocean. The elk were no doubt feeding, and raised their heads at my approach. In daylight, they wouldn't have given my vehicle a second glance. They're used to being gawked at and having cameras pointed in their direction. But things are different now. It's dark, and there may be coyotes nearby. Or cougars.

Once, in the daytime, I crawled on my stomach to a hilltop just above a scattered herd of these resting elk. They were only a few yards away, and I was afraid to move, not knowing how they would react to my being among them. Lying there in the cool grass, propped on my elbows, I spent nearly a half hour observing them, and nothing indicated that they were ever aware of my presence.

I pour myself a cup of coffee and consider taking a walk out to the point. Then I think better of it. I've really been rather lucky these past few months, rambling up mountain inclines and across tangled countryside at night. Aside from my running a few skunks off with tossed rocks, having minor skirmishes with poison oak and stinging nettle, and getting the daylights scared out of me by sudden eruptions of deer and quail, I've done all right. I haven't fallen into a badger hole, been bitten by a snake, or sustained other serious injury. Besides, not only are there mountain lions and coyotes present but the elk themselves can weigh over five hundred pounds and are equipped with sharp hooves and massive antlers. They could strongly object to my violating their territory in the midst of all this blackness.

A great deal of searching can still be done, however. Being out here alone has triggered my hunting instincts. I can maneuver the Trooper to face practically any direction I care to. There are acres of fields and hillsides and miles of lonely roads to investigate on the drive back home.

I try not to encumber myself with any hope for success in finding a mountain lion. For now, the hot coffee tastes good enough, and my headlights burn bright.

My friend, the Zen teacher, once said, "When you drive at night, your headlights don't have to reach all the way to your final destination. They only have to light up what's immediately in front of you."

54

TRAVELING THROUGH
THE DARK

A WEEK AFTER visiting the elk herd, the time seems ripe for another excursion into the night. I feel that it is just a matter of time before I connect with a cougar. If I go out looking often enough, Artemis and Diana, the classic goddesses of the hunt, will be too worn out from watching me to deny me success.

At midnight I slowly retrace last week's route to Inverness and then bypass the Pierce Point turnoff. From here on I'll be heading west, then southwest, along the remote roadway leading to the Point Reyes Lighthouse.

About three miles up the road, near the oyster farm on Drake's Estero, I see a small commotion up ahead. My first thought is that it must be a small whirlwind or dust devil. But the fact is that there's no wind here tonight, an odd situation at this hour in open country so near the coast. As I ease forward, the thing I see appears to be a miniature whirling dervish. I park in the middle of the road, all my truck lights blinking and blazing. A few steps ahead of the front bumper, an animal is racing in tight circles as fast as it can run. I peer down at it in wonder. It is about the size of my thumb, and is called a vagrant shrew. Shrews are the world's smallest mammals. They have what has been described as an "extreme" heart rate. Researchers have recorded as many as twelve hundred beats per minute. The animals, at certain times of the day or night, are highly active. They are voracious predators, and although they're abundant, it's unusual to see one behaving in this manner out in the open.

I'm not knowledgeable enough about shrews to understand exactly what this one's problem is. It doesn't appear to be injured. Nor does it seem to be chasing anything visible. I think of moving it to the side of the road, then remember reading about the razor sharpness of their tiny red teeth and change my mind. (I have also heard that an anomaly of the inner ear can sometimes cause mice and other small rodents to run in circles.)

I climb back in the truck, baffled, as I often am, by what I find while looking for something else.

In my pack are a battered field guide to mammals and some blank sheets of paper. After a little figuring, I work out a rough calculation: it would take approximately 11,428 vagrant shrews to equal the weight of an average mountain lion. With this useless computation in mind, I steer clear of the still-wheeling shrew and continue my drive westward toward the ocean.

Every so often I see deer near the roadside, methodically devouring the grass. The late-night sky is moonless, and without these strong headlights, I'd be driving blind.

Jim Harrison, a writer who, like Borges and James Joyce, is not fully sighted, is also a man drawn to walking and driving at night. In his *Passacaglia on Getting Lost,* he writes, "A trail, other than an animal trail, is an insult to the perceptions."

I am in pursuit of an animal, but this road would certainly not qualify as being anywhere near Harrison's definition of an animal trail. The present path is sinuous, but wholly paved. There's a line down its middle, and its route has been mapped. I'm traveling down a thoroughfare of paint and asphalt that ends only where the earth ends, overlooking the sea.

For some reason, I feel quite sure that I will see no lions tonight, but again the trip has been worthwhile. I'm out here on the edge of things, just a few miles from where I once saw a great blue whale feeding offshore. These whales are the largest mammals ever to have lived on Earth.

Tonight I've seen the whirling shrew, and I'm thinking about great whales. For me, the connecting link between the two—the largest mammal and the smallest—is the mountain lion. I take a Milky Way out of the lunch box and grab my mammal book and pen. By my estimation, it would take 1,733 mountain lions to equal the weight of the blue whale I saw. This is a number I find most interesting, but know in my heart to be of no consequence. The realities of numbers and the lives of wild animals bear no comparison.

With these thoughts idling in my mind, I turn around and begin the drive back. I'm cruising homeward, skimming a long, straight stretch of blacktop at thirty miles per hour, when in my peripheral vision I see a doe and two small spotted fawns begin to cross the roadway ahead of me. I've done enough sailing on San Francisco Bay to recognize immediately the makings of a collision course, and there's no way I'm going to be able to avoid hitting *something*. I stomp the brake pedal hard and hold my breath. Luckily, I do not put the Trooper into a skid, but the relative position of my vehicle and the first fawn remains unchanged. The fawn and I are slowing at the same rate, and I'm sucking in my stomach and practically standing on my toes as I await the hard impact.

The young deer passes slowly beneath the driver's side door and, as I come to a halt, there is a muffled thump against the transmission housing. Before I can start breathing again, I see the little fawn step out from the other side. It shakes its head twice and then scampers back to its mother and the other fawn. It's all I can do to pull over, weakly, to the side of the road.

Sitting here in the darkness, my heart racing, I feel like a fugitive who's been given a reprieve; and in a few moments I'm remembering scattered lines from William Stafford's poem "Traveling Through the Dark." Here it is in full:

Traveling through the dark I found a deer
dead on the edge of the Wilson River road.
It is usually best to roll them into the canyon:
that road is narrow; to swerve might make more dead.

By glow of the tail-light I stumbled back of the car
and stood by the heap, a doe, a recent killing;
she had stiffened already, almost cold.
I dragged her off; she was large in the belly.

My fingers touching her side brought me the reason—
her side was warm; her fawn lay there waiting,
alive, still, never to be born.
Beside that mountain road I hesitated.

The car aimed ahead its lowered parking lights;
under the hood purred the steady engine.
I stood in the glare of the warm exhaust turning red;
around our group I could hear the wilderness listen.

I thought hard for us all—my only swerving—,
then pushed her over the edge into the river.

55

CHANGE OF PLANS

THE NEXT DAY, in a departure from my planned itinerary, I decide to conclude my stint of nighttime driving by performing a marathon, one-night sweep of all the remaining areas on my list combined. I have begun to yearn for diurnal normal-cy. I miss sleeping at night and seeing things in the light of early morning. Yet I wouldn't have missed these nocturnal journeys for the world.

What I have disliked about the drives I've taken, however, is the need to double back on the same roads I've already traveled. In truth, this has nothing to do with my chances of seeing a cougar. It is every bit as unlikely that I'll spot a cougar going out as coming back. But I've always tried to make my move-ments interesting; hiking in broad circles rather than straight out a trail and back, taking roads that allow me to loop back homeward without retracing the same route.

Tonight I plan to make the grandest loop I've made yet on this search, driving over the hill to Fairfax, along the northern slopes of Mount Tamalpais, through Stinson Beach, following the edge of Bolinas Lagoon, past Olema and the Point Reyes headquar-ters, out the Limantour Road and back, and then through Point Reyes Station, around Nicasio, and home. This will cover many, many miles.

For one last time, my oscillating eyes will scan the slowly passing roadsides of the night. These final miles might bring a lucky sighting of the animal I've been looking for so long.

56

THE GRAND LOOP
AND A SURPRISE

THERE WERE FEW other cars on the roadways, and my animal sightings were restricted to the ubiquitous deer and raccoons, and to furtive household pets taking their private leave from nearby residences. At Bolinas Lagoon, a great raft of shorebirds rested on the water, but there was nothing to disturb them. So far, it seemed to be an uneventful night for them as well.

As usual, I drove slowly. I listened to the piano works of Erik Satie and Francis Poulenc. The music, too, seemed quiet and unassuming. I traveled up the coast almost to Point Reyes Station, then headed out toward Limantour; more deer, a few rabbits, much darkness.

By the time I finally reached Nicasio, the community had long been asleep. Not even the telltale bluish glow of a television screen betrayed an isolated occurrence of insomnia.

Not far from here, a friend once reported seeing a ringtail at about this hour, low to the ground and catlike. It took a while for him to recognize it, as it was something he'd never seen before.

The ringtail *(Bassariscus astutus raptor)* is sometimes called the ring-tailed cat, and is an exceedingly rare animal in these parts. Almost all other Marin County sightings have been near the coast, and even these have been uncommon. This relative of the raccoon is truly nocturnal, venturing out only in the deepest period of night, looking for wood rats, insects, and berries. Its long tail shows a dozen or more bands of highly contrasting light-and-dark fur, and its eyes are as large as those of a lemur.

I had never seen a ringtail in the wild, and wondered now if there was a chance I'd ever see one. It wouldn't be the same as seeing a mountain lion, but in some ways its rarity would make it similar.

In other parts of the country, the ringtail is sometimes called a cacomistle, a name derived from American Spanish by way of the Nahuatl word *tlacomiztli*, "the animal that is one-half mountain lion."

Tonight, I would be pleased to find even half of what I looked for.

5 7

DEER ANTLERS

THE ZEN MASTER Hakuin once asked, "In this very moment, what is there to pursue?" And master Dogen questioned, "If you do not find what you're looking for right where you are, where will you find it?"

Whether one looks for enlightenment, mountain

lions, companionship, or untold prosperity, "it" is never far away. A person must be careful of what she looks for, and of what might distract her along the way. The fourteenth-century Buddhist priest Yoshida Kenko, once even warned his followers against picking up deer antlers and smelling them. He noted that these vestigial objects often had a coating of small but adept insects that could enter one's nose and consume one's brain. Though erudite and most insightful, Kenko maintained the belief that a mere sniff of wildness might, by itself, be enough to destroy a person's reason.

58

END OF THE ROAD

THE DUSKY MACHINATIONS that inspired my forays on the road had seemingly come to nothing. "Motorized stalking" had yielded some memorable surprises and an abundance of contemplative time alone, but not much else. I was no closer to seeing a cougar than I had ever been. I began to question, again, whether what I was doing was relevant, whether I was just being a compulsive dilettante, whether I was trying to avoid other issues that might be more pressing.

These drives at night had certainly been a plausible experiment, but I missed the physicality of moving freely on my own. I wanted to be back on the outside of any enclosing walls, in the midst of things, and to walk where I could smell the grass and feel the temperature of the air again. The windshield of the truck had been too much like a television screen, too much like all of the other modern contrivances I was trying to circumvent. I wanted to break loose from all machinery and to escape from the sometimes gut-tightening restrictions of sitting in a motorized vehicle. I wished, once again, to reenter the great world outside and to feel myself dissolve in its unlimited space.

There was something beginning to smolder within me, vague and unrecognized, but just as real and immediate as a finger touching the burner of a hot stove. I was beginning to feel mortified by my lack of success.

Driving home from Nicasio that night, I felt pensive and burdened. After pulling down our dirt road, I parked the truck, shut off the lights, and sat there in the dark. Far from being in an abject state, I still felt like a virtuoso failure. It looked as if my search might be coming to an end. Not only had I chosen the wrong thing to pursue, I had failed to find it. After walking and driving for hundreds of miles, I languished now in my own driveway, oblivious to what was around me and without a valid thought in my head.

Then the thought came. What if, that night, a mountain lion had also been looking for me?

59

JOHN MUIR AND ONE BREATH

AS I SIT on a couch in our living room, with the lights turned off, I can see a few stars through the window, scattered among the tops of the oaks and pines. My wife has gone to bed, supremely patient with both my nighttime preoccupations and my daytime meanderings. She has said it doesn't matter to her whether I find a mountain lion or not, but I'm still feeling like a person with a new car who's just run out of road.

I've been rereading the books of John Muir, trying to learn whether or not he'd ever seen a cougar in his travels. I haven't succeeded in finding an answer to this question, but I have found several inconclusive references to the "California lion" or "panther." Having seen one or not, Muir was certainly aware of this creature's ecological importance. He often stated that an animal needed no other reason to exist other than its own reason. The animal knew perfectly well what it was doing, and it was not up to mankind to determine its worth. He went so far as to say, "Man has injured every animal he has touched." And he felt that observing animals in the wild was one of life's many necessities.

Muir loved walking alone at night, and said that there was no danger in it. He went on to say, "When one is alone at night in the depths of these woods, the stillness is at once awful and sublime. Every leaf seems to speak." He described how one's sense of utter loneliness is "heightened by the invisibility" and how one feels "submerged" in the free expanse of night.

In his late twenties, Muir was temporarily blinded in a freak industrial accident. While working in a carriage factory in Indianapolis, Muir's right eye had been penetrated by the sharp point of a steel file, and sight had quickly drained from it. His left eye had gone into "sympathetic" shock and had also ceased functioning.

This event was the catalyst in Muir's life, changing him forever. For four weeks he was kept in a darkened room, immobile and secluded. Gradually his vision returned, and he was once again allowed to go out walking. He vowed, from that point onward, never to commit himself to any menial pursuit of wages or ambition, but to fully engage himself in studying his environment and learning more of the natural world. A photograph of him taken shortly after this event shows both his worried face and his filmed eye.

Although he had written scattered notes to himself from time to time, Muir now began to keep a journal regularly. For the remainder of his life he was methodical in recording what he did and saw. No impression or idea was unimportant. He seemed to be possessed of a new vision entirely, and began to sing the praises of light. "I know not a single word fine enough for light," he said. He wrote of the "soul" of light, the "glories" of light, the "ethereality" of light, and even compared his own existence to that of "a flake of glass through which light passes." For him, all things in the world were now "different strands of many-colored light." And when he later set eyes on the Sierra Nevada, he renamed this range of mountains "the Range of Light."

Tonight, I consider that I have squandered my time by reading of Muir's many kinds of light when I seem to have so little of my own. I have been unable to discover, even, whether or not he'd ever seen a cougar. I have shoved his books aside so that I can sit quietly and brood about the stars. These scant pinholes in the night sky are light-years away from me, yet I can see them clearly. I am looking directly into the past. Although some of them no longer exist, I can still see their light streaming toward me. Their light brings history into the present. I know that blue stars are younger, and therefore hotter, than red stars. I can follow the calligraphy of their movements and can, by referring to a star map, even find specific stars by name. So why can't I find a cougar? Why can't I see an animal that breathes the same air as I do and shares the same ground? It is illogical and exasperating to think that my search might be as meaningless as the countless years that carry these distant points of light.

I have spent weeks studying blindness, perception, and the dark. I have walked, steeped in the dew of night, wondering about the many elusive things I can't see. I have driven for miles, hoping to see a mountain lion but seeing only tree trunks, brush, broken glass, scattered buildings, deer, elk, raccoons, rabbits, mice, foxes, opossums, and a lunatic shrew.

John Muir said that the power of our imagination was what made us infinite; but emotions are telling me that my own imagination may have led me into a wasteful blunder. I try to distinguish the differences between unrealized ambition and feckless desire. In many ways, I have changed mightily from the man who once sat in front of the nightly news. But something unresolved still bothers me. Perhaps it is merely that I am not yet aware of how *many* things I've learned, of how *many* ways I've changed.

After putting on a sweater, I step outside and take a breath of cool night air. The Zen teachers always said that one breath contains the answers to all our questions. I sit down on the rough planks of our front deck and fold my legs beneath me. Before long, my breathing regulates itself, and I pay it no attention. The night comes into me at the same time as blindness and ambition are expelled. I sit for a long time, maybe for an hour, and then the darkness subtly begins to lean its way toward morning.

PART THREE

MOUNTAINS ARE MOUNTAINS ONCE AGAIN

60

SUNLIGHT

AFTER SEVERAL WEEKS of painting walls and doing home repair, I pack a lunch and venture back up into the hills. Everything seems inordinately bright. There is a beautiful confusion of light and shadow, and even the speckled shadows seem brighter than before. It feels great to be hiking in daylight, and the sun's pure intensity adds to the memory of detail.

The frond of a sword fern casts a shadow like a stepladder lowered across the trail. I've been missing these kinds of visual nuances ever since I limited my excursions to nighttime. Things in the night had been muted; they were either seen or not seen, but there was little room for any subtle shadings or fine distinctions. I would have missed this fern's shadow just as certainly as I had missed the colorations of many wildflowers and the endless shapes and varieties of weeds.

The mountain lions were always somewhere else. Looking for them was like trying to pinch and lift the corner of a shadow; but searching for something specific was liberating, even though the object of the search had begun to feel more and more irrelevant. After all, the lions themselves might just as well have been made out of glass. They appeared to be unfindable. Initially, my commitment to action was what had been of pivotal importance, and I had gradually been transformed from passive observer to active investigator. Traveling my home surroundings had been enormously instructive. From the hills above, I had begun to see where my life was situated. I grew used to seeing our house from different angles. I became curious as to how it was connected with the rest of our community and with the world outside.

During the time I sought translucent cougars, I had also read disturbing reports of the growing ignorance of most of us regarding our own environment. School-age children can recognize nearly a thousand different commercial trademarks, television jingles, and product logos, but are unable to identify the trees that grow in their own neighborhood; the majority of adults have no clue as to where their drinking water originates or where their food comes from; by the age of sixty-five, the average American has spent nearly nine solid years of his or her life watching television.

These reports led to a quiet anomie. I realized that, I too, had experienced some kind of disconnect.

I began taking a closer look around me. I spoke with employees of the water district, visited the local "sanitary" disposal site, began to frequent the local farmer's markets and to meet with organic growers. My wife and I reduced our dependence on outside resources and changed many of our eating habits. We grew familiar with some of the farms where our food was grown, whereas before, we had not even known what *country* it came from.

Gradually, as I took my mountain lion walks, I began to feel more tied in to things. I became more aware of what entered and left the territory. I felt less in danger of living what Wallace Stegner had once termed "the termite life."

To engage in a more "active" kind of looking can be transformative. Regular walking becomes addictive and can lead to something very near spiritual discovery. Our legs and eyes become synchronized in easy rhythm. We begin to notice the minutiae that would probably have escaped us and gone unappreciated. We take delight in finding irregularities, oddments, bits of color out of place.

Today, I have become so absorbed in looking that finding hardly matters. I am like a person in a foreign country who has entered a village he will never see again. I want to take in as much as I can, knowing that the present scene will not repeat itself. Feelings of gain and loss appear simultaneously. Whatever I may ultimately see out on these trails, it is this kind of looking that's grown necessary and that now draws me forward.

WHEN THE CRISIS of John Muir's bout with blindness passed, his sense of purpose was reborn. He reveled in the plain act of looking at things. He began to notice small details he had often overlooked. *Radiant* and *glorious* became his favorite words. When he later began to write in a serious way, his editor and friend, Robert Underwood Johnson, suggested that he control his fondness for *gloriouses*. (Later, Ansel Adams would also speak of "silver light," "arrows of light," and "luminous metallic splendor" when describing the photographs he had taken in the Sierra Nevada. He would often, like Muir, also use the word *glorious* when referring to Sierran light.)

Only now am I beginning to really understand this obsession of Muir's. Walking again in sunlight has me looking everywhere at once, and I feel expansive in a different way than I did when out at night. The freedom of being in darkness has given way to the wonder of being in light, and this contrast magnifies my perception.

61

WRITING IN ANTARCTICA

ONCE DURING a writing seminar, Peter Matthiessen spoke to his students of a problem, very similar to Muir's, that he'd experienced on a recent voyage to Antarctica. Matthiessen always carried a pocket-size notebook with him when he traveled during the day. Each evening he would transfer his field notes into a larger journal, allowing them greater length and detail and putting them into a more structured order. After spending his first day in Antarctica looking at the vast whiteness beyond the ship's rail, he found that he'd written only such notes as "incredible," "splendid light," "unbelievable," "fantastic space." He may well have added several *glorious*es. It is the writer's job, he said, to take these pitifully inept and meager hints of his or her impressions and turn them into something vital, into thoughts and images a reader will never forget.

KALINKA

SOMETIME DURING the protracted course of my nighttime roving, we acquired another cat. Her name is Kalinka. She was feral and is still now half wild. Ever since she arrived at the house, we've had to watch her closely. Still, she seems to be fitting into our life well.

This morning, after a long time being idle, the hinges on my truck door squealed much like a cat in heat, and Kalinka was immediately at the window, looking out. On other days, she can make herself scarce. It would appear that she senses my laserlike attentions. Lately, I've been studying her in every way but through a microscope. She may be the closest thing to a wild mountain lion that I'll ever see, so I'm intrigued by her behavior.

Watching her this closely, however, is probably just a waste of time. I distinctly remember that the French painter Delacroix once wished to do a painting of a tiger. He used his own cat as a model, and this turned out to be an artistic mistake.

No artist should ever substitute one thing for another.

63

ON CAMERAS

WHEN FRIENDS first learned that I was out chasing mountain lions, they seemed able to accept this fact, albeit with some concern for my motives and for my physical safety. What they couldn't understand was my refusal to haul a camera with me. They as much as hinted that, since one could no longer with impunity tote a high-powered big-game rifle through residential neighborhoods, one could at least legitimize this sort of aberrant behavior by carrying along a camera. Furthermore, they were inclined to say that if I succeeded in finding a lion, no one would believe me unless there was a substantiating photograph to prove it. I found this unduly pessimistic.

I remembered traveling alone on my first trip to Europe. I'd brought along a camera that was as heavy as a brick. I only took four or five snapshots on that trip and could easily have purchased better photographs from any postcard rack. I voiced my regret for bringing this camera with me to the people of nine different countries. It was cumbersome and unneeded, I said. They only nodded. On my way back to California, I stopped over for a few days in New York City and happened to pick up a copy of the *Christian Science Monitor* that contained an article by the writer Paul Theroux. It began, "It is my good fortune that I've never owned a camera."

Theroux went on to tell of travels in Italy and in Kenya, and of how his not having a camera had sharpened his own observational skills. Looking closely at things and then describing them carefully seemed a perfect exercise for a writer. Every camera had a mind of its own. It often saw things in a different way than even a professional photographer might see them.

Many times in my own experience I'd missed a good look at a hawk or squandered a coyote sighting by reaching for binoculars when I didn't need them. It was a purely reflexive action, and now I didn't want to spoil my chances of seeing a mountain lion by fumbling with a camera case. If I saw a cougar, I would always have the memory, and I wanted to prolong the experience as much as I could, without interruption.

One can develop the art of looking just as certainly as one can master the art of playing the violin. Theroux compared the freedom of traveling without a camera to the adroitness of riding a bike without using one's hands. And even after all these years, it still seemed like good advice.

6 4

DEVELOPMENTS

MANKIND HAS OFTEN concerned itself with capturing the momentary aspects of nature. The first photographs were made in the early nineteenth century, but they were themselves fleeting images. One could only observe these pictures by candlelight, and for just a few minute's time, before they'd disappear. In these early stages of development (as it were), there was no way for a photographer to fix these images in time or to make them permanent. (This changed in 1839 with the invention of the daguerreotype.)

Zen students and photographers have much in common. Both are acutely visionary, concerned with the practicalities of light and darkness, perception and clarity. The pursuit of either of these practices demands that those involved first find what's truly significant in their lives before they can ever hope to turn this significance into something that can be seen by others.

LAKOTA

FULLY AWARE of the shortcomings of capturing images on film, I set out today, camera in hand, on my way to take the photograph of a live cougar. After all the mystery and doubt of the past many months, I'm in a splendid mood. This one is a sure thing.

Rob and Barbara Dicely live in the next county. They do not live what most of us would call a life of convenience. They live on twenty-two acres of rolling woodland with a mountain lion named Lakota. They also share their residence with three cheetahs, two African leopards, six Canadian lynxes, three Siberian lynxes, two bobcats, two snow leopards, one clouded leopard, two caracals, one serval, and an ocelot. The Dicelys have run a business called Leopards, Etc. out of their home for the past sixteen years. They appear together at about 150 events each year, in front of schoolchildren, park and recreation departments, scouting groups, and other organizations, where they attempt to educate those present on the significance and current standing of the great cats of the world. All of the Dicely's animals were born in captivity and would never be able to survive on their own in the wild. Their surroundings, here in this natural setting, are both peaceful and impeccable.

I had, since my first days of lion chasing, been eager to speak with someone who lived with a cougar every day. I couldn't imagine the uncommon luxury of a person who could step outside their door and see one of these animals whenever they wished.

To see Lakota in the light of early afternoon is a stunning experience. She radiates power and unconcern. She was born in Oregon and has lived here with the Dicelys since she was twelve weeks old. She is now nine years of age, entering what, for captive cougars, would be considered her "middle age." She doesn't play with the abandon she did when younger, but she's still bright and strong. Her weight is a shade over a hundred pounds. She avoids direct eye contact with people but can become "riveted" on any object that captures her attention. She's immensely strong for her size. Often, when walking her on a leash, Rob must offset her will to go forward by pulling her firmly in an upward direction. This upward angle is just enough of an edge to prevent Rob from being dragged behind her. When taken outside, Lakota appears more relaxed whenever she is visiting new and different surroundings. She is often anxious and more irritable when being walked about on her own home ground.

Even with Rob holding her securely, it is still rather unsettling for me to discover this animal in my viewfinder. The zoom lens brings her face even closer, although I'm not much more than an arm's length away. My proximity causes her to become restless, and soon she complains. I make one last exposure before slowly backing away.

ON THE DRIVE HOME, I take a quick glance at the camera sitting on the seat next to me. There may or may not be a mountain lion inside the camera, but the true animal will forever remain outside. Lakota was keenly aware of every movement I made in front of her, but never once would she look directly into the camera's eye.

66

ONE AMONG MANY

MY LION WALKS have grown more casual. I'm going out in the field less often, and I try to concern myself with other things. Today there is a ceiling of scattered low clouds, and young turkey vultures wheel through them, appearing and disappearing at their leisure.

But then, before me in the drying mud, I come upon a single mountain lion track, surrounded by a flurry of prints made by two large dogs. I look for another cougar print but can find no others nearby. This has me puzzled until I realize what must have happened. The cougar had been here first; then the excited dogs came upon the scene, smelled the lion tracks, and went haywire. They had run in circles, leaping over one another, until they obliterated all the lion tracks but one. This lone mountain lion track was the only evidence that the animal had been here. I'd nearly walked past it; but once truly seen, this mark was as distinct as a smudged thumbprint in the middle of a page of printed text. It was impossible to miss it.

I spend another hour poking around within thirty yards of this embossed mud print, looking for further indications of the mountain lion. Then I give up. The track is probably three days old. It may as well have been made a lifetime ago.

The clouds grow heavier, and the soaring birds disappear for good.

67

SOSAKU

IT WAS ABOUT this time that I began to transfer my own jotted field notes into writing of more intelligible form. This exercise seemed to help me organize my thoughts and to review my past actions; but when I looked at page after page of scribbled words, I found that a great many of them didn't make much sense. It was not only the hurried quality of some of the writing (especially that done in the dark), but also my own inability to express my thoughts.

There is a Japanese word, *sosaku*, which has two different meanings. Written with one set of characters, it means "to search"; in its other form, it is defined as "to write" or "to write creatively." To search for something tangible, and to look for the correct word to describe it, are often nearly the same thing. Tracking an animal and writing about it may merely be two different ways of arriving at the same conclusion.

68

CHEMISTRY

RARE ANIMALS are difficult to find and nearly impossible to keep. Wild animals are, by definition, unpredictable and can revert at any time to behavior that might threaten their keepers. Human beings, on the other hand, are conscious of the divide between their wild beginnings and where they are today. Early ferocity has gradually given way to socially acceptable behavior, and savagery has been abandoned in favor of more efficient and creative ways of achieving desired results. One must always balance instinct, passion, and strong will with social considerations and collective concerns. In this way, wildness and culture blend into a system that works both for the society as a whole and for the individuals in it.

Of course, things can go awry. Domestic sheep are known to carry a pneumonia virus that is 100 percent contagious and always fatal to the native, undomesticated bighorn sheep born in the wild. And human violence can suddenly erupt in the most quiet of cities, among normally cultured people. Civilized ways of life and wildly divergent inclinations are often at odds, yet they are forever intermingled. Our daily lives have become an amalgam of propriety and wildness.

This morning I read Judith Larner Lowry's writings on seed propagation, and I was reminded of that mandatory, nearly failed chemistry class I took years ago when students were taught the correct ways of diluting several common acids. Certain acids, such as sulfuric acid, could be diluted by simply mixing them with water, but one had to combine them in the right way. If you slowly poured the acid into a beaker of water, you would successfully dilute the acid. However, if you reversed this order and poured the water into the acid, an explosion might occur. Although these two processes were remarkably similar, it was absolutely necessary for us to remember what made them different.

These days, I seem to be mingling even more slowly with what's outside. As I enter the wilder areas of the countryside, I am conscious of the changes encountered when I go from the companionship of society into a pure and undiluted landscape. The rules of the game are altered, and I can sense a different atmosphere. The small and diminishing wildness within me seems to take heart from my need to enter an even greater wildness outside.

69

THE DEGREE OF HUNGER

YESTERDAY WAS so long that the birds stopped singing early and went home to bed.

After the long semi-isolation imposed by winter rains, the warmth of spring and summer brings a renewed awareness of one's neighbors. Even though I've started walking the high ridges again, it's difficult to escape the cacophonous symphony of leaf blowers, chain saws, weed cutters, and framing hammers coming from the valley below.

I sit on the trailside, making a few notes about the

stubborn qualities of pine pitch. My fingers seem to stick to the paper as I write.

Far across the canyon, a roughly worked seam of burgundy-barked manzanita appears to bind togeth-er the wrinkled sky and the drying field of hillside grass beneath it. The mud here has already turned to dust in places, and the cirrus clouds offer no promise of further moisture. These blue days are a welcome change from the lackluster grayness of the many weeks past.

The ridge I'm sitting on is well removed from any major trail, and ridges like this are growing hard to find. Most of these high lands are riddled with fire roads, water tanks, transmission towers, and the like, and each year brings more difficulty in finding a for-gotten elevation, such as this one, that's been left alone.

Tracking in loose dust can be every bit as produc-tive as tracking in mud or snow. But today, on this exposed ridge, the slight breezes that brought in the cirrus clouds are just strong enough to blow a moun-tain lion's tracks to pieces. Rather than searching down below where there is more cover, I decide to hold my ground.

I fold myself into a more formal sitting position, straighten my spine, and within ten minutes, I'm nearly asleep in the full sunlight. There is no Zen teacher here to observe me. There is no cougar to fol-low. I feel my consciousness slowly slipping away and beginning to disappear.

Then I jerk wide awake again. I suddenly remem-ber being in this spot a year earlier. The grass was a tad more verdant then, and the sky more troubled. I had found a lion-killed deer just below this ridge, and it was the first of these I'd ever discovered. There was disorder at the back of the deer's neck, but the head, front shoulders, and forelegs were untouched. The rear two-thirds of the animal was mostly lost, and what was left was strewn with dirt and strands of grass. It was an odd sight, disarming but in no way repulsive. It was a scene combining neatness and disarray, and it offered a view of starkly naked consequence coupled with a responding, and nearly demure, attempt to cover it.

The creation of such a scene was dependent upon a variety of coinciding factors: the lay of the land, the time of day, the awareness and physical condition of the deer, and the cougar's strength, determination, hunting skills, and degree of hunger.

To bring down a deer, a lion almost always carries out a two-stage attack: an artful approach followed by a most audacious charge. The approach begins the instant the big cat sees its prey. The cougar usually crouches as low to the ground as possible, and then, using every bit of possible cover, advances toward its target with the utmost care. It seems to absorb the silence of the surrounding rocks and grass as it moves forward, often crawling on its belly for a hundred yards or more. It never stops watching its quarry. When it is near enough, within seventy-five feet or so, the cougar will wait for the moment when the deer is most unguarded. Then the cat will launch itself into the open, into an extravagant, unrestrained, and momentous charge toward the only other thing that exists on the earth, this deer.

These time-consuming efforts often end in failure. The deer has evolved right along with the lion in its ability to stay alive. Its senses are acute, and it has explosive speed, agility, and uncommon vision of its own. Any bungled attempt on its life will be an invaluable lesson for the deer, and these lessons will accumulate as the deer grows older. The lion will briefly consider what went wrong, and then continue working on her skills, stalking birds, rushing through fallen leaves.

The image of a year ago, the one-third of the deer I'd found near here, gives way once again to the quilted landscape of the present. I feel like a person visiting the scene of a great battleground, a pilgrim who's wandered into Gettysburg or Wounded Knee years later. This place where I'm sitting was, at one time, an arena of violent death, a theater that held at least one final performance. I wonder what else might have occurred here. I wonder how things can be so peaceful now. And I wonder how many other eyes might have looked down from this same place, seeking some kind of answer.

70

ABBEY'S ARROW

IN TIME, as I crisscrossed the countryside, engaged in my solitary pursuit, I became more confident of my own capabilities and resourcefulness. My route-finding abilities grew much more precise, and my tracking skills improved greatly. I was a long way from being a professional tracker, yet I was somehow able to hold my own and even found relaxation in the process. I enjoyed being able to plot my own course of action and to find my way to a specific destination and back again. Sometimes I would follow established routes and trails. At other times, I would venture across untraveled wildlands or into remote areas where I could easily have become lost. I began using the compass in an almost casual manner, and would often merely glance toward the sun to orient myself. I read shadows as easily as another person might have read a well-worn bus schedule; and I followed bent-down grass as another person might follow the painted lines of a highway. I liked the feeling of, usually, knowing where I was.

Of course, at times none of these abilities worked. I would bumble my way into a dead-end canyon or onto an unclimbable face of loose rock. There were unforeseen chasms and muddy bogs. At times I could only turn around, retrace my steps, and take pleasure in the fact that my foolishness had not been seen by anyone else.

Although these coastal mountains lack the objective dangers of higher and more rugged ranges, they have periodically been cause enough for people to become lost and die. And thousands of people have sustained lesser injuries while hiking here.

The world-renowned cellist Pablo Casals was hit by a hurtling boulder while descending Mount Tamalpais by way of the Throckmorton Trail. He was knocked from his feet; his left hand was mangled, and his career as a musician was nearly brought to an end. (Oddly enough, his first thought was one of relief: "Thank God, I'll never have to play the cello again!")

While on a winter walk along the edge of Cataract Creek, the famed botanist Alice Eastwood slipped on wet moss and fell into the raging waters. A companion was able to rescue her downstream, and just kept her from being swept down the mountainside.

These kinds of close calls have never been uncommon; so I always exercised care when negotiating any new route. I tried to be alert to anything that appeared to be out of place. I followed the signs in front of me, and pursued anything unusual that called to me, no matter from what direction.

In his essay *The Great American Desert,* Edward Abbey spoke of having come upon one such sign as this, a sign that demanded a great deal of time for him to comprehend. He'd been exploring an arduous passage on the far side of a formidable mountain in Arizona and had worked his way up to a difficult summit. Feeling certain that no other person had visited this place before, he was amazed to find an arrow made of carefully placed stones there on the ground before him. The arrow pointed off into the far distance, and Abbey took its direction and walked where it indicated. He soon came to a ledge that was the last step before a long, five-hundred-foot drop. Certainly this was not what the arrow pointed to. There were many other cliffs like this on the surrounding mountainside. He went back to where he'd found the arrow and looked intently again toward the horizon. He still saw nothing. There was absolutely nothing there. And this was when Abbey realized the singularly important reason for the arrow; it pointed to nothing but the empty desert and the silent world. This was its meaning. It pointed to the place where nothing was. It pointed nowhere.

ZEN BASEBALL

ARGUABLY, THE MOST important Zen document dealing with emptiness or nothingness (a major
theme in Zen study) is the Heart Sutra, a compilation
of hundreds of volumes of Mahayana Buddhist text
reduced to a single page. This short page contains
the very essence of Zen philosophy and is recited
daily by Zen followers throughout the world. It is
the arrow that points to the heart of practice and
understanding.

To look in the direction of nothingness is one of
the aims of meditation. To *see* this nothingness, even
briefly, is often reason enough to break out the
noisemakers and lose everything one has gained by
reveling in false celebration.

To seek something solid, like a mountain lion,
would seem to be an easy task when compared with
trying to find the great emptiness that enfolds all
things of the universe. Yet modern physics seems to
be proving the teachings of the Heart Sutra to be
true. The things we see in this world *are* empty.
They are composed of atoms, and atoms are almost
entirely without substance. The volume of an atom is
one million billion times larger than that of its nucleus alone, and what is not the nucleus is void. If a
simple atom could be enlarged to the size of Yankee
Stadium, its nucleus would be about the size of a
sesame seed. The rest is emptiness, and this is the
way the world is made. (In baseball, there really is no
such thing as a "hit." Both the ball and bat are made

of atoms and therefore empty. The atoms of both bat and ball possess like negative charges and thereby repel each other. Without these negatively charged fields, both objects would pass through each other untouched.)

To arrive at true nothingness, one must be led in every possible direction at once. One must follow every arrow, every baseline, even when they lead nowhere.

ROUTE FINDING

IF ASKED TO place the point of a pencil near the middle top edge of this page and to inscribe a line downward through the text, without touching any printed word or letter until the wide bottom margin of the page is reached, most people would be able to do so. But few, if any, of these lines would follow the same course. There are so many choices and alternatives available in this exercise that each person would simply rely upon his or her own impulses. Route finding would be a personal matter. Each person, without thinking about right or wrong, would create their own path. This is freedom. But there is another freedom which might be considered even greater: writing words on a blank page. In 1934, A. S. J. Tessimond put his pencil to paper and wrote the following lines: "Cats, no less liquid than their shadows, offer no angles to the wind. They slip, diminished, neat, through loopholes less than themselves."

Sometimes, in the conscious effort of traveling from point A to point B, we can encounter a whole new world. When we walk off the trail, we walk off the map. It's a way of turning one page and beginning another. This may be why mountaineers, after considering a seemingly endless array of travel options, decide to climb one distant summit. And it just may be why I'm trying to find a mountain lion in places I've never seen or gone before.

73

THE FAWN

THIS IS A HILL I've probably climbed fifty times before. The day is clear and not unpleasant, but the trail I'm on is in a remote area and is a route unknown to most casual hikers. I doubt if there's another person within several miles.

For reasons I can't explain, I suddenly begin to feel uncomfortable. Perhaps it's the sunlight or residual fatigue. I'm standing in the middle of the trail, trying to catch my breath, when something on the very outside limit of my peripheral vision rushes out of sight behind me. I turn quickly to see what it is, but can see nothing out of place. There are only short weeds and scrubby brush, a few young fir trees, and a roughly piled pyramid of loose rocks. There is only the empty trail I've traveled on to get here.

I feel alone, exposed, and stupid. Everyone knows you shouldn't hike by yourself in rugged country, and I've been getting away with it for far too long.

But what did I see? I turn in a slow three-sixty, looking intently at everything around me. There's no sign of any other animal life whatever. It must have been something I imagined. How could anything be that fast?

TWENTY MINUTES LATER, I find a dead fawn on the trail ahead of me. A delicate thread of blood stretches across the path and seems to tether her neck to a nearby shrub just as securely as if she were being held by a length of rusted wire.

Another unexpected feeling comes over me. I know I should investigate this death further, but for some reason, on this particular occasion, I cannot. Like a person who has mistakenly entered the scene of a crime, I walk quietly once around the remains, leaving everything untouched, and then continue moving up the long trail ahead.

For an hour afterward, I walk through something unexplained, a kind of miasmic haze. I feel like someone who belongs somewhere else. The Buddhist sutras say that, in reality, a bucolic scene is no different from the view inside a slaughterhouse; they are each a kind of dream, shallow and provisional. But the poet Masaoka Shiki said, "I was wrong about Zen. I thought it taught us how to accept death; but instead, it teaches us how to live fearlessly in any circumstance."

74

LEWIS CARROLL

THE IMAGE OF the dead fawn has stayed with me for several days. Zen students are usually counseled to leave such things behind.

Although I've studied Zen for many years now, I am clearly not one of the illuminati. Enlightenment, like so many things in life, has cleverly eluded me. Now I've taken my meditation on the road, and feel somewhat bewitched by my own sense of motion. I take simple pleasure in merely observing the passing world. Everything about me has renewed relevance, and nothing is trite; but this is not enlightenment. There is no way to hold this heightened condition still, no way to capture it even for a single moment. A man or woman can no more enlighten himself or herself than a candle can will itself to ignite. Revelation grows stronger as it waits in the shadows and will appear in its own time. But sometimes, as in the writings of Lewis Carroll, we are left with only the fading radiance of the cat's smile, long after the cat itself has disappeared.

75

NATURE LOVES TO HIDE

"NATURE LOVES to hide." This is another of the succinct observations made by the Greek philosopher Heracleitus. And if there is a phrase that better sums up my current relationship with cougars, I haven't found it.

Nevertheless, one remarkable fact began to emerge from my explorations. Although the cats I looked for remained at large, more of their tracks, scats, and scrapings were being discovered within close proximity of human dwellings, parking lots, and city streets. Much of the harder evidence was left uncovered, with a seeming lack of concern for its discovery. This was highly unusual.

Mountain lion expert Dr. Paul Beier conducted a series of studies in southern California that yielded surprising information on the lion territories there. Although most biologists believed that the animals were being driven farther and farther away from human encroachment, Beier's research, using radio telemetry, showed that the cougar's territories were not expanding outwardly after all but were being integrated even more secretly into the human-occupied world. Cougars passed beneath freeways and visited man-made structures routinely. This was, in some ways, a hopeful sign.

But as Hemingway once said, the land ages quickly once we come. Historically, whenever the human family has appropriated a new landscape, other large animals have suddenly vanished. Most predators are killed, and the survival skills of those remaining are tested as never before. The arrival of guns and well-trained hunting dogs almost guaranteed that mountain lions, after being resident since before recorded time, would become extirpated.

These days, things have changed considerably. Most modern families who buy homes do so without any necessity of deforesting hillsides, planting crops, or ambushing marauding animals. The demand for more land, however, continually moves people outward, and encounters with wildlife will almost certainly become more commonplace.

The fact that I find lion tracks not far from a crowded convenience store is not, perforce, some signal warning of impending danger, but more likely an indication that there may be fewer places for some animals to hide.

76

ARTEMIS

WITH A CROOKED screwdriver, I am chiseling away at my boots; digging between the rubber lugs, scraping the soles, trying to rid them of the accrued mud I've brought home from the trail. The clay is sun-hardened and more tenacious than one might think. Even in this simple act, I find places that are unreachable.

It is a good day to work outside, the air warm and still, the jays chasing each other lazily from one level of greenery to another. Not far from where I'm sitting are patches of bunchgrass, Douglas iris, and California poppy. These native plants must continually compete with the increasing numbers of invasive species that my wife and I, when feeling motivated, pull and cut and cart away.

As I try to get my boots in shape for the day's work, I mull over some recent information I've acquired from a new gardening catalog. *Dandelion*, it turns out, means "lion's tooth," because of its sharply indented leaves. This was something I'd never thought of before. And later in the catalog, there came an even bigger surprise. After pages of descriptive text regaling the merits of garden rakes, kitchen composters, flower seeds, and bat guano came a page extolling organically produced pest repellents. One could, for just ten dollars and ninety-five cents, secure eight ounces of fox, coyote, or bob-cat urine. These substances were said to discourage everything from mice to woodchucks. When it came to thwarting deer, ammunition came in a heavier form. There were preparations made from the ammonium soaps of fatty acids, putrefied eggs, and generous servings of cayenne pepper extract. But the capstone to this displayed assortment was an elixir known as "glandular lion extract," a deer repellent with "authority." Readers of the catalog were warned that using this product might possibly attract mountain lions to their yards and gardens if lions lived nearby.

With the edge of my hand, I brush the loose crumbs of excavated mud and dirt from our redwood deck and then take another look at the flat area between the bunchgrass and the poppies. Artemis, the Greek goddess of the hunt, was also a splendid botanist. She gathered and named a wide variety of plants as she searched for animal tracks atop the soil. "Enjoy the flowers," she would say, "but observe the ground between the flowers as well."

77

DRAWING LESSON

RECENTLY, MY DAYS have coalesced. One day slowly becomes another. And as the receding days become overshadowed and distanced from one another, they are hidden inside one another like a nested set of Matryoshka dolls. Lately, I've felt my dedication to this lion search beginning to waver, and I find difficulty in keeping my vision and motivation fresh. Still, I enjoy the long walks, and I've taken to studying plant life and the properties of certain kinds of stones. It is so refreshing, after all this searching, to be able to look at something that's not trying to run away. Gradually, I seem to have given up on ever finding a cougar, but there are so many other things to enjoy that I feel no real sense of loss. Even now, almost accidentally, I do occasionally run across signs of a lion. As in the past, these sporadic traces are the only evidence that the cats are here.

Somehow, this morning—far off the trail and in the loose dirt of a newly excavated gopher hole—I've found another of these infrequent mountain lion tracks. In the top pocket of my pack is a flat six-inch-square piece of clear Plexiglas. This is not a Zen map. I lay the transparent square carefully over the cat's track and trace the outline of the impression with an erasable marker. This outline is, in turn, transferred to a sheet of paper and stuck temporarily in my thick notebook.

This notebook is twice the size it once was. Those first twenty words, chosen at random and written so long ago, have been joined by countless scribbled notes, maps drawn in the field, newspaper clippings, park brochures, postcards, tracings, and pages torn from organic gardening catalogs. There are notes on the stars, on quantum physics, on trails that have washed out, and on the lateness of certain flowers. The book has grown nearly too large and too heavy to carry, but it is almost always the first thing I put in my pack. It seems to give me purpose when, in the midst of uncertain days, what I do seems questionable. Somewhere in the middle of all this collected rummage may lurk something of value.

On a nearby rocky knoll, pleased again at having found a single track, I decide to celebrate the day by eating lunch early. For a backrest, I wedge the day pack hard against a Tertiary rock, and then lay out fruit and sandwiches. In front of me, I have nothing less than the Pacific Ocean to look at. The sea is flat and calm this morning, and I wonder whether it might not be time to take another boat trip soon. After all this sporadic prowling, it might feel good just to escape the land for a day.

Leafing through my notebook, I come across Melville once again. In chapter 42 of *Moby Dick,* he tells us that all things we see before us are "subtile deceits." The blank page and the whale Ahab seeks are both white, not so much a color as a radiant expanse of wildly disorganized light. What is there that is visible that we can trust?

A lone gull glides overhead and then alights to sit and watch me eat my lunch. Perhaps this is also just another deceit come dressed in whiteness. If so, this particular illusion seems content to wait there patiently until I come to my senses and toss out a bit of bread crust.

A sandwich sits, half covering the tracing of the mountain lion track I carefully collected earlier.

With this recent drawing in mind, I raise a bent forefinger and carefully trace the bird's outline in the air.

78

BERKELEY

GARY SNYDER and I are sitting in a small East Indian restaurant on University Avenue in Berkeley. He is stirring a packet of sugar into his hot chai with the blade of his Swiss army knife. He is a man who prefers his own tools to the plastic implements the restaurant leaves out for us.

Gary and I don't see each other often, and this meeting is a rare opportunity. Both of us happen to be in Berkeley on independent tasks, and it's a good occasion to get caught up on things. The conversation slips easily from current family news to updates on the health of mutual friends, the present status of several California wildfires, sustainable forestry, the difficulties of translating Buddhist texts, and the ethereal qualities of coho salmon. After we are filled with the hot and spicy tea, Gary asks whether I've found my mountain lion yet. The blank look on my face gives him his answer.

He then tells me a story. Two weeks earlier, two of his close neighbors were visited by a cougar. The couple owned a dog, and the dog made the fatal mistake of rushing directly toward the lion. After the briefest of confrontations, the dog was killed and carried down the hill. The neighbors had witnessed the entire event. They went looking for their dog and found it the next day, partially eaten and scantily covered with dirt and leaves.

My only response was that this must have been devastating.

"Students of dharma take every opportunity to closely study the matters of life and death," Gary said. "These people are Tibetan Buddhists, and when they realized there was nothing they could do to save the dog, they tried to observe the event dispassionately and with clear-eyed vision."

"All the same," I replied, "it's a much easier lesson to learn when you see it happening to someone else's dog."

Outside in the sunlight, we walk awhile and talk a bit further. I tell him of my recent readings on "emptiness" and the gradual merging of new scientific theory with traditional Buddhist thought.

"Emptiness is often only a metaphor," Gary says. "Both Zen teachers and physics professors are trying to describe experiences and events that can't be seen or explained. In order to do this, they have to come up with a new language."

"But it does make you think," I say. "My looking for a mountain lion could also be taken as metaphor, but I don't see it that way. It's much more tangible to me than the possibility of wormholes in the universe, superstring connections, or one hand clapping. But I can understand being surrounded by emptiness. There's so much vacant space in this sidewalk we're walking on that it's a miracle we don't fall right through."

He looked at me and laughed. "Don't worry, my friend. We're all just walking on water."

79

SUNFLOWERS

AFTER SO MUCH wandering about, I had finally grown more easygoing in my ambles through the
countryside. In my walking, there was no semblance
of any existential quest. The French writer Antoine
de Saint-Exupery once said that the essential things
in life always remain invisible to the eye, and I'd
found this, generally, to be true.

The nature of mountain lions centers on their
secretiveness. They are reticent and discreet, and
they withhold themselves from the rest of the world.
They spend much of their time asleep in hidden
places, and their peregrinations are measured in
meticulous stalkings and extravagant bursts of
speed. Their success depends on being able to do all
of these things well, and I decided, after all this time,
that I would leave them alone and let them have
peace. Certainly, if a lion had ever seen me scouting
between the trees, searching for clues of its where-
abouts, its first response would have been annoy-
ance. The fact that I hadn't been attacked seemed
bizarrely considerate, given the circumstances.

In most kinds of field research, even the slightest
contact between the observer and the object
observed can alter the character of both. Great
amounts of research have been riven by encounters
that were too close or too subjective. I had found
that a lack of contact, even of visual contact, could
also lead one to a lasting effect. Paradoxically, I'd
begun to feel that I knew the lions much better for
having not found one. There was an almost per-

verse pleasure in realizing how well they had avoided me.

In the place of lions, there were other pleasures to be found instead: the strengthening of one's body in steady exercise, the acquisition of a new skill, the memory of a sound discovered in the middle of the night. Innumerable epiphanies were at hand once the decision was made to go in search of something. The lions had not materialized, and now they were immaterial in an even greater sense; I had practically let go of any interest I had in finding them.

I felt that I had come to a crossroad; and that, even though the path ahead was indistinct, the words I'd written had formed a trail of a different sort. Like footprints, they had left a visible record that extended back to the very beginning, to that list of twenty unplanned words I'd written first. Whether I'd untangled meaning from them wasn't clear, but they had served as a starting point. After all these months, they left a track down the middle of the page that was both thought-provoking and indecipherable.

I was glad to still have these twenty words, and the ragged pages of words that followed them. Being able to see this history contained, even in a disordered fashion, was helpful. The ensuing record of the chase had become wedded with the search itself. Not only had the action and the writing been joined, but they seemed to have created one another.

Did van Gogh create the sunflowers, I wondered, or was it the flowers that made Vincent what he was? One could argue these questions unceasingly, but could conclude at last only that he had somehow found his inspiration. His searching had been expressed in something extraordinarily visual, something as tangible as color and light can ever be. Yet his paintings remained elusive. The reasons for their existence seemed unimportant. Such mysteries as these are often best left unconsidered, Vincent said, for when the head conquers, the heart usually dies.

80

THE WATERFALL

TODAY IS ONE of those days when one can almost sense a change in the air. I rouse myself after business chores to take another walk out to Devil's Gulch. The surrounding hills interpose themselves between me and any potential breeze; but high above, the turkey vultures wheel as ever on unseen thermals and then nearly spiral out of sight.

I feel wearier today than usual. The eagerness I once felt about what I was doing has turned into something else. After all the up-and-down walking and emotional rises and falls, I feel resigned to the fact that I might go on this way forever, walking these hills, looking fervently at whatever might present itself.

I cross a rustic wooden bridge and veer up a smaller trail eastward, traveling along the verdant edge of Devil's Gulch Creek. I know that there is little chance of seeing a cougar here, but taking this trail is, more than anything, a symbolic gesture. I feel that this may be my last walk for a while. The trail ahead meanders freely for quite a ways and then dead-ends at a small rock face and cascade known as Stairstep Falls. There's no other way out of here, and this too is symbolic. One reaches the end of the trail, turns around, and goes home. This is exactly where I feel I need to walk today. I would like to be physically stopped from even vaguely considering mountain lions any further. This is where the long trail will end.

I can hear the creek streaming past on my left, and look to see a few steelhead fry facing valiantly upstream. They know where they are headed, even if they are going nowhere.

There are vast tangles of coffee berry, gooseberry, poison oak, hazelnut, currant, and wild rose all along the way. A few juncos fan their tails and flit in and out of the understory. Oaks and Douglas fir tower overhead. Soon I forget what trail I'm on and where I'm headed. This is so enjoyable, moving over this ground without having much of anything in mind.

By the time I reach the waterfall, my energies have lifted. There is not much flow coming down the rock face, but what comes is steady and unceasing. I stand as close to the falls as I can get without becoming drenched by the creek. It reminds me of being back in the *zendo*. I focus my full attention on this wall of moving water, and every so often I'm tapped on the shoulder by something trying to awaken me—a swaying branch, say, or the cold touch of errant drops of water.

As I look at this cascading wall, I sense another change taking place; this may not be my last walk after all. I'm no longer confused about the reason for all my walking or for my continued preoccupation with mountain lions. *It's all just part of living!* That's all! Life creates its own reasons for being alive. Soon my entire search seems to be tipping and rolling down the rock face. Water tumbles over the high edge of the cliff and washes away the Halloween masks, sea voyages, rattlesnakes, blindness, ambition, ravens, elk herds, tracking classes, Zen monks, recurrent dreams, spinning shrews, field notes, directional compasses, misperceptions, eyeglasses, pencil stubs, muddy boots, and all the other detritus of the world. All of nature seems to be traveling concurrently through liquid darkness and light. The mountain lions have truly disappeared. Everything else is walking on the water.

81

RAINWATER

WHEN I SAT DOWN to write the account of this waterfall experience in my notebook, I discovered that the book's binding was nearly coming apart. The covers had been worn through in places and were greatly soiled. The loose pages of this tattered journal reminded me of a story I'd once heard.

Late in the year 1840, a hefty collection of music manuscripts was put up for auction in Germany, and through strange circumstances, this lot happened to include the original handwritten draft of Mozart's Rondo in A Major. The man who had purchased this material, in his ignorance, had unfastened the pages of these variously bound portfolios and framed some of them as wall decorations. Other sheets of the manuscript had been cut into quarter-pages, placed in envelopes, and sent to friends as greeting cards.

Word of this dissection and dissemination was

later announced to the music community, and for many years afterward a dedicated group of music scholars and historians worked diligently, trying to bring the pages back together. They were eventually able to resurrect Mozart's rondo and present it to audiences in its original, intended form.

I wondered about the pieces of my own life, and the elements of the search I'd been engaged in. I wondered if inspired scholarship could make sense of the loosely floating pages that described my past couple of years.

I remembered, then, another story; one from my own past that had long ago been forgotten. It had been an occasion that had changed my way of thinking and perhaps even my way of life.

I'd been newly married to my first wife, and we had been invited to spend the weekend at a friend's rented house in San Francisco. This home was owned by the mother of the experimental composer Henry Cowell, and was quite unique. It was situated in a quiet residential neighborhood, and although it appeared unobtrusive from the outside, it had been designed by Frank Lloyd Wright. The interior walls were covered in a fabric resembling jute, and there were shelves, tables, and benches that could be pivoted upward into these walls and hidden.

After spending the first night, we woke very early the next morning, and fatefully, I picked up a book resting on the bedside table. It was a copy of *Silence*, autographed and inscribed to Mrs. Cowell by her friend John Cage. I was suddenly lost in reading, not only for the morning but for quite a long time thereafter.

Cage, a man who was later known as "the apostle of indeterminacy," was a composer who would purposely cut his own manuscripts into pieces and then rearrange them. He avoided any sense of rationality in the composition of his works, and developed what is known as aleatory music—music composed by fate, chance, and accident. He was also involved in the then-arcane arts of Zen Buddhist study and mushroom hunting, both of which interested him for the rest of his life, and which also dealt with chance.

But it was the ease of his storytelling that most appealed to me. Even when cut apart and peppered with a dozen different type styles, his prose conveyed a genuine, natural, and friendly wisdom regarding whatever subject was at hand. He rejoiced in happenings the rest of us would consider as discouragingly irritating. He reveled in last-minute twists of events, sudden surprises, abrupt noises, and canceled plans brought by rainy days. He preferred the unstructured and the unanticipated; and later, even well into his last years, he seemed to be made more buoyant by not knowing what would happen next.

All of this was perhaps a dangerous influence on someone in their early twenties, but I then recognized it as being nothing short of real truth and practicality; the reliance upon the events of the present moment, the absurdity of building castles in the air. It would be unfair of me to blame John Cage for the failure of that first early marriage, but I wish I'd read his book before the ceremony, the rite in which my wife and I had promised each other that things would be more or less predictable until the end of time.

And as it turned out, this was one of the last times we were ever to see our friend, the one who had asked us to stay with her that weekend long ago.

She had been born into wealth but was orphaned by the time she started school. At five years of age, she had been placed in the care of foster parents and had lived with them until she finished high school and left to begin her college education. The day after her twenty-first birthday, the day she was scheduled to receive her inheritance, she received a business letter from her stepparents, along with a packaged, itemized bill for the entire cost of her upbringing; every hairpin, every Kleenex, every tube of peppermint toothpaste, and every birthday gift for the past sixteen years was accounted for and reimbursement demanded. She was being billed for all her upbringing.

Her lawyer appeared dumbfounded. And, without ever having held it, she watched her inheritance disappear into her past. It was a shock from which she never recovered. It seemed to her that her entire life had been reduced to a regimen of cold record-keeping, and there wasn't one spontaneous gesture, one act of loving kindness, that hadn't been a calculated effort by her new parents to increase their future worth.

The highly detailed pages of her economic history seemed to tear her life apart, and there was no one who could bring things back together for her. Shortly after we visited her, we learned that this young woman had suffered a rare, catastrophic medical emergency, and had died.

SEATED NOW, next to this shaded trail between the trees, holding on to my pages of hastily written words, I wonder about the value of our life and of our time. I have no more thoughts of mountain lions. But I think again of John Cage. . . .

I was fortunate enough, finally, to meet him just a few years before his death. I was visiting New York on business, attending a book publisher's meeting in one of the upstairs rooms of the Algonquin Hotel, and Cage was there. During the course of conversation, he told a story that I'll never forget.

It seems that an apprehensive friend of his was about to take his first trip to India, to study Buddhism, and had asked Cage what he should do. Cage had advised his friend that during his stay in India, he should always pretend that he was dreaming.

When the friend returned from his travels, he called John Cage on the telephone and told him about his trip. He said that his plane had landed in Delhi and that they had sat for a long time on the tarmac, waiting for an arrival gate to open. As they sat there, the friend had looked out of the plane's window and seen a naked man and woman and their two naked children, all squatting next to the runway, drinking with their cupped hands from a pool of rainwater.

"It was exactly like being in a dream," he said.

AND NOW, these people, and these lions, are bound into my life's pages.

ENVOI

ONCE, WHEN THE Zen master Tokusan was still a student, he visited his teacher, Ryutan, just before sundown. They sat on the floor of Ryutan's hut, casually drinking tea and discussing Zen until deep into the night. At last Ryutan said, "Maybe it's about time you went home." Tokusan bowed to his teacher and walked to the door. "It's completely dark outside," he said. Ryutan lit a lantern and said, "Why not take this?" Just as Tokusan was about to take the lamp from his teacher's hands, Ryutan blew out the flame. Tokusan suddenly knew everything there was to know.

Enlightenment stories such as this one highlight the dramatic results of Zen study but tell you nothing of the years of preparation that preceded them.

Sometimes there is no remedy for our situation other than to begin from a point of absolute darkness. Turning off a television set and extinguishing a lantern have certain similarities; they are both abrupt and transition making, and can leave us in a different world. In darkness, we are always on our own.

When I clicked off the TV news so long ago, I really had no idea what I was going to do next, but I knew that I had to get moving. Watching television had been wearisome, and the thought of looking for something that didn't want to be found was greatly appealing to me. I knew that looking for a wild cougar would be a haphazard enterprise and that my inexperience would make any logical daily progression out of the question, but by keeping a written record of what I encountered, I hoped to give some purpose to my endeavor and to help organize my random thoughts. I had no real idea how difficult this kind of writing could be; it was at least as difficult as the search itself. Clearly, trying to put my thoughts on paper offered many more ways to fail than it did to succeed. Writing was like entering a minefield filled with incendiaries. The Zen teachers were right; words are dangerous.

Out on the trail, however, I found that most of these fears were soon forgotten. I began to chase words with the same enthusiasm with which I had chased the lions. And, as finding the animal became more doubtful, my choice of words became more critical. I began to look at writing as something much closer to the heart than mere note-taking.

MY COUGAR STUDIES evolved over a period of approximately three years; and eventually, after all my looking, I found them.

I spotted two different mountain lions, on separate occasions, each walking casually and seemingly unconcerned in daylight. After three years of looking, the total viewing time allowed to me amounted to less than twenty seconds. I considered myself then, as I do now, extremely fortunate to have seen them at all.

As an added bonus, I nearly collided head-on with a third lion as I drove home from vacation, in the dead of night, across the flatlands of western Nevada.

The irony of this third encounter would have pro-voked uproarious laughter in any Zen master who ever lived.

ACKNOWLEDGMENTS

FINDING A mountain lion, the way I did it, is an awkward, dogged, and solitary pursuit. And even if one were to possess exceptional good fortune, this kind of search is always hampered by the radical deportment of the lions themselves. To attempt to determine what a lion is going to do next is a hopeless task. Without dogs, treeing one or making one hold still is out of the question.

However, it must be said that if my long search was strictly a lone endeavor, the writing of this book was not. I owe a great deal to those who went before me, and to many others who walked with me in spirit, especially my wife, Lura, and my friends and family.

I would also like to thank Rob and Barbara Dicely, Gary Fellers, Rick Hopkins, the late Rick Fields, Ginny Fifield, Steve Torres, Terry Jenkins, Jill Giel, Doug Padley, Lanny Waggoner, Jerry Maracchini, Ken Logan, Rita Green, Gary Snyder, Ed Brown, Peter Matthiessen, Taigen Dan Leighton, Harley Shaw, Chris Healy, San Stiver, Stephanie and Kathleen Budros, Chris Alexander, Jennifer Rivera, George Lane, Peter Elias, Paul Beier, E. Lee Fitzhugh, and the staff members of the Hornocker Wildlife Institute, Point Reyes Field Seminars, the Mountain Lion Foundation, and the Marin County Chapter of the California Native Plant Society.

Thanks also to my literary agent, Victoria Shoemaker, to copy editor Miranda Ottewell, and to George Gibson and Jackie Johnson at Walker & Company in New York.

SELECT BIBLIOGRAPHY

When weather conditions (either external or internal) made hiking and tracking impossible, I did a great deal of reading. The following books were immensely helpful and encouraging:

Abbey, Edward. *The Journey Home: Some Words in Defense of the American West.* New York: E. P. Dutton, 1977.

Alderton, David. *Wild Cats of the World.* London: Blandford, 1998.

Alinder, Mary Street. *Ansel Adams: A Biography.* New York: Henry Holt, 1996.

Barrow, John D. *The Book of Nothing: Vacuums, Voids, and the Latest Ideas about the Origins of the Universe.* New York: Pantheon, 2001.

Biddle, Wayne. *A Field Guide to the Invisible.* New York: Henry Holt, 1998.

Borges, Jorge Luis. *Selected Non-Fictions.* New York: Viking Penguin, 1999.

————. *Selected Poems.* New York: Penguin, 2000.

Bova, Ben. *The Beauty of Light.* New York: John Wiley & Sons, 1988.

Busch, Robert H. *The Cougar Almanac.* New York: Lyons & Burford, 1996.

Cleary, Thomas. *Secrets of the Blue Cliff Record.* Boston: Shambhala, 2000.

Cole, K. C. *The Hole in the Universe: How Scientists*

Peered over the Edge of Emptiness and Found Everything. New York: Harcourt, 2001.

Colinvaux, Paul. *Why Big Fierce Animals Are Rare*. Princeton, N.J.: Princeton University Press, 1978.

Danz, Harold P. *Cougar!* Athens, Ohio: Swallow Press/Ohio University Press, 1999.

Ehrlich, Gretel. *John Muir: Nature's Visionary*. Washington, D.C.: National Geographic Society, 2000.

Emerson, Ralph Waldo. *Essays and Lectures*. New York: Library of America, 1983.

Evens, Jules G. *The Natural History of the Point Reyes Peninsula*. Point Reyes, Calif.: Point Reyes Natural Seashore Association, 1988.

Ewing, Susan, and Elizabeth Grossman. *Shadow Cat*. Seattle: Sasquatch Books, 1999.

Fairly, Lincoln. *Mount Tamalpais: A History*. San Francisco: Scottwall Associates, 1987.

Ferris, Timothy. *Coming of Age in the Milky Way*. New York: Anchor Books, 1989.

Gifford, Terry, ed. *John Muir: His Life and Letters and Other Writings*. Seattle: Mountaineers, 1996.

Greene, Brian. *The Elegant Universe*. New York: W. W. Norton, 1999.

Guggisberg, C. A. W. *Wild Cats of the World*. New York: Taplinger, 1975.

Halfpenny, James. *A Field Guide to Mammal Tracking in North America*. Boulder: Johnson Books, 1986.

Hall, E. Raymond. *Mammals of Nevada*. Reno: University of Nevada Press, 1995.

Halpern, Daniel, and Dan Frank. *The Nature Reader*. Hopewell, N.J.: Ecco Press, 1996.

Hansen, Kevin. *Cougar: The American Lion*. Flagstaff, Ariz.: Northland, 1992.

Hubbell, Sue. *Shrinking the Cat: Genetic Engineer-*

ing before We Knew About Genes. New York: Houghton Mifflin, 2001.

Jameson, E. W., and Hans J. Peeters. *California Mammals*. Berkeley and Los Angeles: University of California Press, 1988.

Kaplan, Robert. *The Nothing That Is: A Natural History of Zero*. New York: Oxford University Press, 1999.

Keene, Donald. *Essays in Idleness: The Tsurezuregusa of Kenko*. New York: Columbia University Press, 1967.

Kleiman, Devra G. *Wild Mammals in Captivity*. Chicago: University of Chicago Press, 1996.

Lowry, Judith Larner. *Gardening with a Wild Heart*. Berkeley: University of California Press, 1999.

McCullough, Helen Craig. *Classical Japanese Prose*. Stanford, Calif.: Stanford University Press, 1990.

McGinniss, Joe. *Going to Extremes*. New York: Alfred A. Knopf, 1980.

Malin, Shimon. *Nature Loves to Hide: Quantum Physics and the Nature of Reality, a Western Perspective*. New York: Oxford University Press, 2001.

Matthiessen, Peter. *The Snow Leopard*. New York: Viking Press, 1978.

Melville, Herman. *Moby Dick*. Berkeley and Los Angeles: University of California Press, 1979.

Miner, Earl, Hiroko Odagiri, and Robert E. Morrell. *The Princeton Companion to Classical Japanese Literature*. Princeton, N.J.: Princeton University Press, 1985.

Muir, John. *Nature Writings*. New York: Library of America, 1997.

Murie, Olaus J. *A Field Guide to Animal Tracks*. Boston: Houghton Mifflin, 1975.

Peat, F. David. *The Blackwinged Night: Creativity in Nature and Mind*. Cambridge, Mass.: Perseus Books, 2000.

Perkowitz, Sidney. *The Empire of Light*. New York: Henry Holt, 1996.

Peterson, David, ed. *A Hunter's Heart: Honest Essays on Blood Sport*. New York: Henry Holt, 1996.

Rezendes, Paul. *Tracking and the Art of Seeing*. Charlotte, Vt.: Camden House, 1992.

Richardson, Robert D. *Henry Thoreau: A Life of the Mind*. Berkeley and Los Angeles: University of California Press, 1986.

Rowell, Galen, and Michael Sewell. *Bay Area Wild*. San Francisco: Sierra Club Books, 1999.

Schaller, George B. *The Serengeti Lion*. Chicago: University of Chicago Press, 1972.

Sekida, Katsuki. *Two Zen Classics: Mumonkan and Hekiganroku*. New York: Weatherhill, 1977.

Shaw, Harley G. *Mountain Lion Field Guide*. Phoenix: Arizona Game and Fish Department, 1979.

———. *Soul among Lions*. Boulder, Colo.: Johnson Books, 1989.

Shepard, Paul. *The Only World We've Got*. San Francisco: Sierra Club Books, 1996.

Shirane, Haruo. *Traces of Dreams: Landscape, Cultural Memory, and the Poetry of Basho*. Stanford, Calif.: Stanford University Press, 1998.

Snyder, Gary. *A Place in Space: Ethics, Aesthetics, and Watersheds*. Washington, D.C.: Counterpoint, 1995.

———. *The Practice of the Wild*. San Francisco: North Point Press, 1990.

Suzuki, D. T. *Zen and Japanese Culture*. Princeton, N.J.: Princeton University Press/Bollingen Foundation, 1959.

Tanahashi, Kazuaki, ed. *Moon in a Dewdrop: Writings of Zen Master Dogen*. San Francisco: North Point Press, 1985.

Thomas, Elizabeth Marshall. *The Tribe of Tiger: Cats and Their Culture*. New York: Simon & Schuster, 1994.

Thuan, Trinh Xuan. *Chaos and Harmony: Perspectives on Scientific Revolutions of the Twentieth Century*. New York: Oxford University Press, 2001.

Torres, Steven. *Mountain Lion Alert*. Helena, Mt.: Falcon, 1997.

Turner, Alan. *The Big Cats and Their Fossil Relatives*. New York: Columbia University Press, 1997.

Walker, Evan Harris. *The Physics of Consciousness*. Cambridge, Mass.: Perseus Books, 2000.

Young, Stanley P., and Edward A. Goldman. *The Puma: Mysterious American Cat*. New York: Dover, 1964.

INDEX